Beautiful
Quilling
Step-by-Step

Beautiful Quilling
Step-by-Step

JANET WILSON, JANE JENKINS, DIANE BODEN CRANE & JUDY CARDINAL

SEARCH PRESS

First published in Great Britain 2010

Search Press Limited
Wellwood, North Farm Road,
Tunbridge Wells, Kent TN2 3DR

Based on the following books published by Search Press:

Quilled Wild Flowers by Janet Wilson, 2008
Three-Dimensional Quilling by Jane Jenkins, 2007
Miniature Quilling by Diane Boden Crane, 2007
Quilled Borders & Motifs by Judy Cardinal, 2008

ISBN: 978-1-84448-510-9

The Publishers and author can accept no responsibility for
any consequences arising from the information, advice or
instructions given in this publication.

Readers are permitted to reproduce any of the items in this
book for their personal use, or for the purposes of selling
for charity, free of charge and without the prior permission
of the Publishers. Any use of the items for commercial
purposes is not permitted without the prior permission of the
Publishers.

Suppliers
If you have difficulty in obtaining any of the materials and
equipment mentioned in this book, then please visit the
Search Press website for details of suppliers:
www.searchpress.com

Conversion tables

Strip width

Most of the measurements in this book are given in
both metric (millimetres) and imperial (inches) units.
The widths of the paper strips used, in metric units,
range from 4cm to 0.5mm. Their approximate imperial
equivalents are as follows:

0.5mm	$^1/_{48}$in	1.5mm	$^1/_{16}$in
1mm	$^1/_{24}$in	2mm	$^1/_{12}$in
3mm	$^1/_8$in	5mm	$^3/_{16}$in
8mm	$^5/_{16}$in	6mm	¼in
10mm	$^3/_8$i	15mm	$^5/_8$in
3.5cm	$1^3/_8$in	4cm	$1^5/_8$in

Strip length

Throughout this book, strip lengths are given as
fractions of a full-length strip, as detailed below:

1 strip = 450mm (18in)

$^1/_2$ strip = 225mm (9in)

$^1/_3$ strip = 150mm (6in)

$^1/_4$ strip = 112mm (4½in)

$^1/_8$ strip = 56mm (2¼in)

$^1/_{16}$ strip = 28mm (1¼in)

Mark your quilling board with these lengths as a quick
reference. It is not necessary to measure each strip –
simply fold the strip into half, quarter, etc. and cut.

Publishers' note

All the step-by-step photographs in this book
feature the authors Janet Wilson, Jane Jenkins,
Diane Boden Crane and Judy Cardinal demonstrating
quilling. No models have been used.

Contents

Quilled Wild Flowers

by Janet Wilson

Quilling appears to have started in religious houses in Mediterranean countries around the fifteenth century. Gilded decorations for holy pictures and reliquaries were normally gifts from rich people in return for absolution from sins. Poorer religious communities devised a similar effect using gilded strips of paper wound into filigree shapes round a quill pen. The gilded paper was probably stripped from the edges of their Bibles and missals. These shapes were used to make wide borders round the reliquaries and pictures.

By the seventeenth century quilling was used in place of more expensive paintings to decorate walls. Coats of arms were surrounded by wide borders made from tiny pieces of wound paper. Regency ladies decorated fire screens, tea caddies, furniture and screens. Jane Austen wrote in her book *Sense and Sensibility* that Lucy was quilling a filigree basket. The Brontë sisters were also quillers. The Pilgrim Fathers took the art of quilling to the New World and American museums have examples of early candle sconces, boxes and pictures decorated with quilling.

I started quilling in the mid-1970s and as the interest in this art form took hold, the Quilling Guild was formed. As with all arts and crafts, fashions come and fashions go but I am delighted to see that quilling is once again enjoying popularity with a new generation.

Nature has the most wonderful array of subjects, and to walk through a wood or meadow full of wild flowers is to walk through one of nature's art galleries. In this chapter I have tried to reproduce the delight and beauty of some of our wild flowers, some sadly close to extinction. Enjoy reproducing some of nature's gems in the gentle, ancient art of rolling paper.

All the features of this wild flower sampler can be made using the patterns from the projects or the variations that follow them. The patterns for the variations can be found on pages 184–187.

Materials

Basic equipment

For every project in this chapter you will need the following:

A cork quilling board I recommend you make a clear plastic sleeve to go over your quilling board; this enables you to slip the pattern under the plastic and glue the shapes or designs together on top of it. Your work will not stick to the plastic thus making life much easier. Use a clean plastic bag, slit it down the sides, wrap it round your quilling board and secure it with strips of low-tack tape. When you get too many holes in the plastic, you can move the sleeve round to a fresh area.

Pins Pearl-headed pins are easier to get hold of and are my choice for securing pieces of quilling on your board.

Quilling tools I have mainly used a needle tool for the projects in this chapter. This is a long-eyed needle from which the very top of the eye has been snipped off. The point of the needle is then placed into a needle vice. These tools can be purchased ready-made. If you make your own, snip off the end of the eye inside a bag to avoid injury to your eyes if the end flies off. The other tool used is a fine quilling tool, with a small diameter head.

PVA glue A tacky glue is better as it gives a virtually instant bond. Do not put too much out on to your glue tray (I use the plastic lids from drums of sauce granules) as it dries out quickly.

Cocktail sticks These are the very best way to apply tiny dots of glue to closed coils. They can also be rolled in the glue to spread it on to the back of your quilling before sticking it to the project.

Tweezers Curved tweezers make assembling your projects easier.

Scissors High-quality, fine-point embroidery scissors are best for fringing papers and snipping tiny points.

A quilling board, PVA glue, quilling tools and cocktail sticks, tweezers, fine embroidery scissors and pearl-headed pins.

Rotating craft table

This is ideal for quilling, though not essential. The cutting mat that comes with the table can be removed and the quilling board put into the recess. Not only is the angle of the board much better for your eyes, but the board can be rotated to enable you to put your designs together without having to hold your hands at odd angles. This makes winding huskings much easier.

Quilling papers

Ready-cut strips of quilling paper are widely available in a whole array of different colours. The 3mm wide papers are the most frequently used, and they are stocked by a large number of shops. The 2mm, 5mm, 6mm or 10mm wide papers and the gilded edge papers are available from more specialist paper retailers. This chapter uses 3mm and some 2mm and 5mm wide strips as well as gilded edge papers. Generally speaking, soft quality quilling papers do not hold their shape very well, whereas if the paper is too stiff it can be more difficult to shape, so examine quilling strips carefully so that you get just the right paper for you, one that is easy to shape and holds the shape. The right quality strips are also fairly good-natured as they usually allow you to change a shape without trace!

Paper and cards

The gift bags and boxes in this chapter are constructed from metallic or pearlised card and are available in a large range of colours. The greetings cards used for projects are all ready-made and come in packs of four or five available from local craft shops. Tracing paper (90gsm) is ideal for helping you get your quilling in the right place on your project.

Permanent marker pens

Professional quality markers have been used to shade leaves and flowers. Place the pieces to be shaded on to the plastic sleeve of your quilling board and gently apply the colour.
   If you do it after you have assembled your design on the project, you run the risk of getting colour on the project as well as the quilling.

Blanks to decorate

Box blanks, with recessed panels are ideal for quillers. Use gesso primer on them first and then paint them in a colour or colours to tone with your quilled project.
   Glass paperweights with recesses are also great for mounting your quilling into. Alternatively, recycle glass air fresheners. Remove the remains of the gel, wash the glass container in hot soapy water and it is ready for use.

Other materials

Crimper Quilling strips can be fed through a crimper to produce a zigzag effect. They can then be used to decorate projects (see the sampler on pages 6–7).

Shaper board Some quilling boards come with a plastic shaper on one side. This enables you to make coils of exactly the same size and is a must for making eccentric coils (see page 14).

All-purpose clear adhesive This was used to stick the quilled design to the glass base in the Speedwell project (see page 30).

Fringing machines Mechanical fringers are expensive but if you do a lot of fringing, they are worth the money.

Ribbon slot punch, hammer and mat The ribbon slot punch comes with different heads and unlike a hand punch it enables you to make the slots anywhere on your project. Use with a hammer on a dedicated cutting mat.

Ribbon This is used to decorate the Scarlet Pimpernel gift bag (see page 42).

Ruler This is for measuring but also to help you place double-sided tape in a straight line (see the Scarlet Pimpernel project, page 42).

Craft foam pads These are good for supporting a 'floating' element such as the butterfly wing in the Sweet Violet project (see page 36).

A crimper, all-purpose clear adhesive, fringing machines, shaper boards, ruler, ribbon slot punch, hammer and mat, ribbon, craft foam pads and double-sided tape.

Perforating mat Use this with a pin and tracing paper to prick out patterns on projects.

Double-sided tape I have used super sticky 3mm (¹/₈in) tape, ideal for sticking decorations to projects.

Glue lines These make it less fiddly to construct boxes and gift bags if you are making your own.

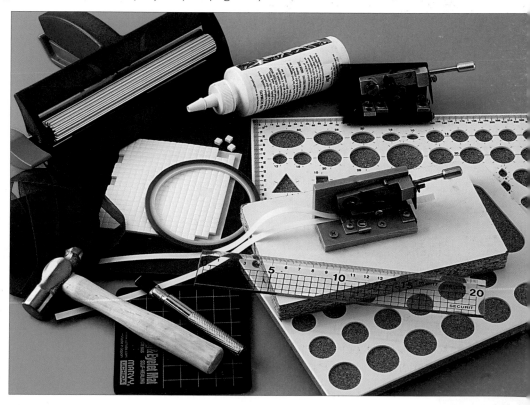

Basic techniques

Closed loose coil

Once the basic coil has relaxed, a tiny dab of glue is applied to close the coil which can then be made into the required shape.

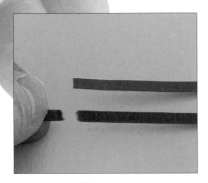

1 Pinch the end off the strip. This will make it easy to blend in later, unlike the untorn strip shown at the top.

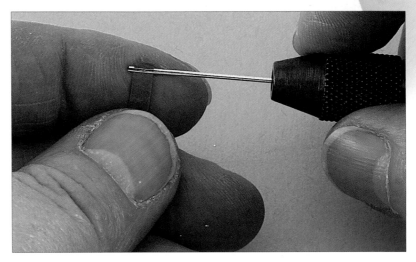

2 Feed the end of the strip through the slot in the needle tool.

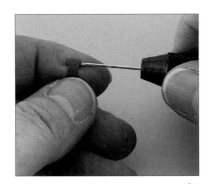

3 Turn the needle tool to begin rolling the coil. Keep turning until you have rolled the whole length of the strip.

4 Drop the completed coil from the needle tool as shown.

5 Use a cocktail stick to place a blob of glue on the end of the coil.

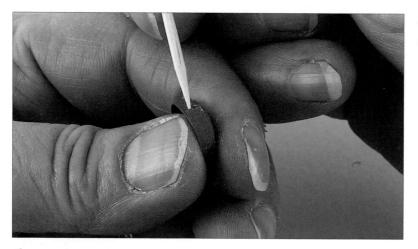

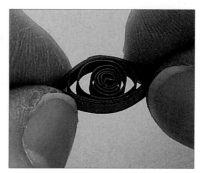

6 Close the coil and use the cocktail stick to blend in the end so that the join does not show.

7 Pinch the edges of the coil to squeeze it into an eye shape.

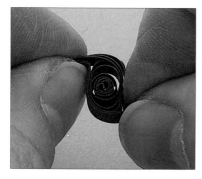

The finished leaf-shaped closed loose coil.

8 Shape the coil further to create a leaf shape.

Open coil

An open coil is achieved by allowing the coil to relax when you drop it from the needle tool instead of gluing down the end. Open coils are usually placed inside a quilling design and allowed to open out within the space.

Eccentric coil

Here a rolled coil is dropped into a circle on the shaper side of the quilling board. A pin pulls the centre down to the open end of the coil and glue is applied to fix the off centre in place. Once dry, an eccentric coil can be shaped like a closed loose coil.

1 Make a coil and drop it into a circle on the shaper board.

2 Put a pin into the centre of the coil.

3 Gather the centre of the coil tightly against the edge and push the pin into the board.

4 Use a cocktail stick to rub glue between the pin and the edge of the coil.

5 Take the pin out and shape the coil into a petal shape with your fingers.

The finished petal-shaped eccentric coil.

Peg

Pegs are for flower centres and for other design elements such as the ladybird's head and spots (see the Lesser Celandine project on page 22).

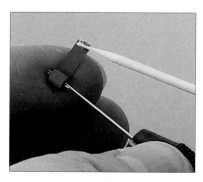

1 Make a coil, rolling tightly until you are almost at the end of the strip. Place a little glue on the end using a cocktail stick.

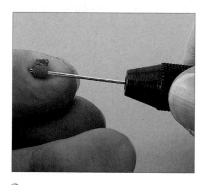

2 Continue rolling tightly to the end of the strip.

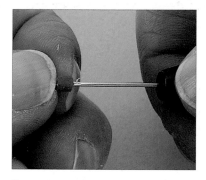

3 Ease the coil off the needle tool with your finger and thumb.

The finished peg.

Fringing

The most popular application is for making flowers rolled in the same way as for a peg. Fringe your paper by hand using embroidery scissors or use a fringing machine.

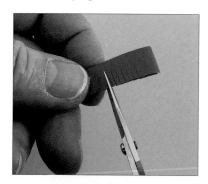

1 Fold a 10mm strip in half and then in half again. Cut into each folded end using fine-pointed scissors and then fringe the strip.

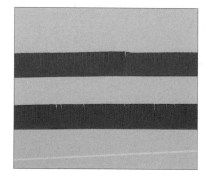

Here the hand-fringed strip (top) is shown with a strip fringed by machine.

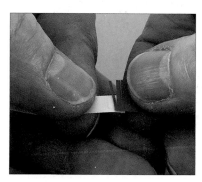

2 Glue the end of a 5mm yellow strip to the end of the fringed piece.

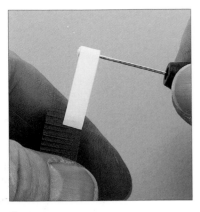
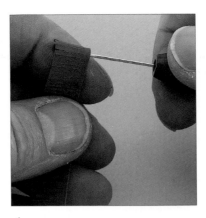

3 Begin rolling the yellow strip into a peg.

4 Continue rolling the fringed strip.

5 Use a cocktail stick to place a blob of glue on the non-fringed side of the strip at the end.

6 Close the fringed flower, take it off the needle tool and use a pin or your thumb to open up the fringe.

The finished fringed flower.

Filigree shapes

No glue is used in the making of these delicate shapes. The finished shapes can be used in many different ways.

S shape

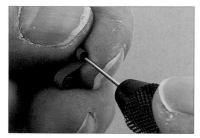

Roll one end of the strip, then roll the other end in the opposite direction.

C shape

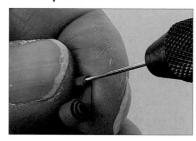

Roll both ends of the coil in the same direction.

The finished S and C shapes.

Fronds

1 Fold a strip to create a V shape with ends of differing length.

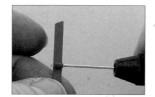

2 Use the needle tool to roll down one end.

3 Roll down the other end in the same direction.

The finished frond shape.

Heart

1 Fold a strip in the middle to make an even V shape.

2 Roll down each side to face the middle as shown.

The finished heart shape.

Huskings

This method dates from Georgian times and can be used for large, unusual shapes, with or without a collar.

Collared husking

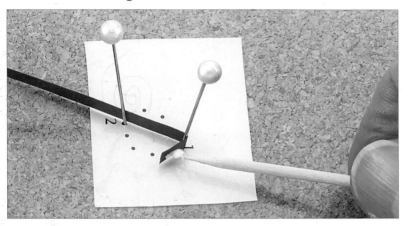

2 Bring the strip round 2 and 1, then back up to 2.

1 Place the pattern for the petal under the plastic of the quilling board. Put in pins 1 and 2. Hook one end of the strip and place it round the pins as shown. Use a cocktail stick to put a little glue on the end.

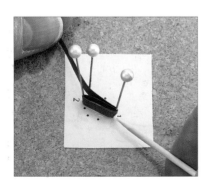

3 Put in the third pin to the right as shown. Add more glue at point 1.

4 Take the strip round the third pin and back to 1.

5 Place the fourth pin to the left as shown and take the strip round it. Add more glue at point 1.

6 Go back round pin 1, place the fifth pin to the right, take the strip round it. Add glue at point 1 and take the strip round it.

7 Put in pin 6 to the left, take the strip round it and add glue at point 1.

8 Take the strip round 1, put in pin 7 to the right, take the strip round it, add glue at point 1 and take the strip round it again.

9 Add the eighth pin on the left and take the strip round it. Add glue at point 1 and take the strip round it.

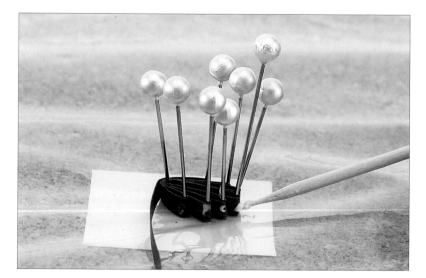

10 Add a little glue to each of the tips on the left-hand side of the husking as shown.

11 Bring the strip round to enclose the husking.

12 Add glue to the right-hand tips. Bring the strip round to measure how much you will need to fully enclose the husking. Tear off the excess.

13 Add glue at point 1 and at the torn end of the strip.

14 Close the husking and use a clean cocktail stick to blend in the end.

The finished collared husking.

Uncollared husking

The finished uncollared husking.

An uncollared husking is made in the same way; however you do not enclose the husking with the strip at the end, but close it as shown.

Wheatear

These are ideal for long leaves, as in the Bluebells project on page 48. You can loop them by hand, use a wide-toothed comb, or use a quilling board and pins as shown here.

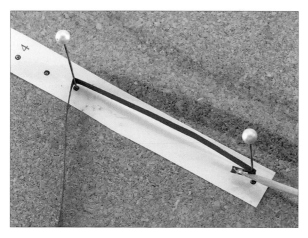

1 Start with two pins. Hook the end of a strip round pin 1. Take the strip round pin 2. Place a blob of glue on the hooked end of the strip at pin 1.

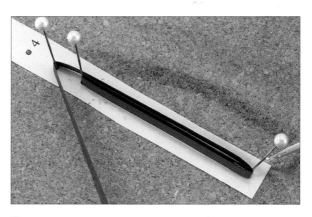

2 Take the strip round pin 1. Add a third pin as shown and take the strip round it.

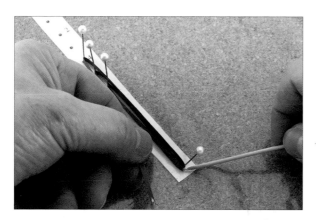

3 Add glue at pin 1 and go round it, then add a fourth pin and take the strip round it. Tear off the excess. Add glue to the end and at pin 1. Close the end.

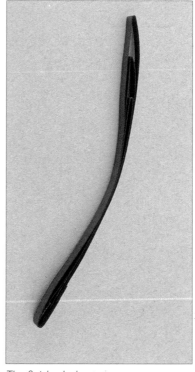

The finished wheatear.

Lesser Celandine

The lesser celandine (*Ranunculus fascaria*) is a member of the buttercup family that grows in woods, grassland, alongside streams and as a garden weed. It has been used by herbalists to treat scrofula and more recently, haemorrhoids. The poet William Wordsworth wrote: 'There is a flower, the lesser celandine/That shrinks, like many more, from cold and rain/ And, the firm moment that the sun may shine/Bright as the sun himself, 'tis out again!' The card in this project shows a two-spot ladybird visiting the plant.

You will need

- Basic equipment (page 8)
- A5 folded card
- Tracing paper
- Quilling papers:
- 2mm green for stems and leaves
- 3mm bright yellow for petals
- 3mm soft green for flower centres
- 3mm red for ladybird wings
- 5mm bright yellow for fringed flower centres
- 3mm black for ladybird's head and spots
- Pine permanent marker

The pattern for the Lesser Celandine quilling, shown full size.

Pin placements for leaf huskings.

Leaf 1   Leaf 2   Leaf 3

1 Fringe a 7cm (2¾in), 5mm wide yellow strip. Use a spot of glue to stick a 2cm (¾in), 3mm wide soft green strip to the end.

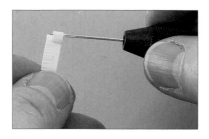

2 Use the needle tool to roll the green strip into a peg.

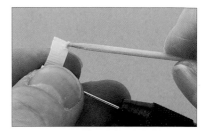

3 Continue rolling to roll up the fringed part and glue the end to close the flower centre.

4 Place the pattern under the plastic of your quilling board. Place the flower centre as shown and put a pin in the centre.

5 Make seven closed loose coils using 5cm (2in), 3mm wide yellow strips. Leaving the joins at the bottom, pinch the tops to make petal shapes.

6 Glue the rounded end and the edge of each petal so that it sticks to the next petal. Place all the petals using tweezers.

7 Take out the pin and fluff out the fringed centre using a pin.

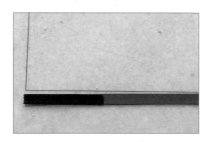

8 To make the ladybird's wing cases, stick a 2cm (¾in), 3mm black strip to a 5cm (2in), 3mm wide red strip.

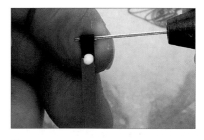

9 Place a dot of glue on the join and roll the black strip into a peg.

10 Wait for the glue to dry, then roll the red strip into a loose coil. Drop it from the needle tool and let it relax.

11 Use glue to close the coil and blend the end using a cocktail stick. Repeat steps 8–11 to make the other wing case.

12 Shape each wing case into a half circle with your fingers.

13 Pin one wing case on the board. Glue the side and push the other wing case against it with tweezers.

14 Pin the other wing case to the board to keep it in place while the glue dries.

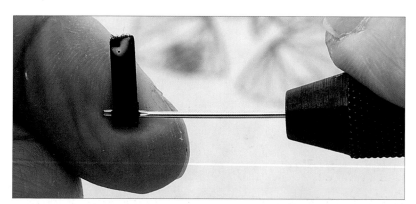

15 Make a peg for the ladybird's head using a 5cm (2in), 3mm wide black strip.

16 Glue the side of the peg and stick it to the ladybird's wing cases.

17 Photocopy the pattern for leaf 3 and place it under the plastic of your quilling board. Make a collared husking with 2mm green strips, leaving a length of strip at the end for a stem.

18 Trace the pattern. Place the card with the tracing on top of the perforating mat and prick through the flower centres with a pin to mark their position.

19 Make all the flowers and leaf huskings, following the pattern. Leave long stems on the leaves. Roll a glued cocktail stick over the backs of the flowers.

20 Stick the flowers down using the pattern and the pricked holes as a guide.

21 Position the leaves, glue the ends of the stems and trim them.

22 Make flower stems with 2.5cm (1in), 2mm wide green strips. Snip one end of each.

23 Separate the ends as shown and glue them using a cocktail stick.

24 Position the stems as in the pattern and press the glued ends into the flowers with tweezers.

25 Roll glue onto the back of the ladybird using a cocktail stick and position it as shown.

26 Use the pine permanent marker to add shadows for a three-dimensional effect.

The finished Lesser Celandine greetings card.

The Lesser Celandine design has been reused here without the ladybird, to decorate a small handmade gift bag which could be used for a wedding favour. (See template on page 185.)

In this version of the pattern, extra flowers have been added to create a more intricate greetings card. (See template on page 186, bottom.)

Speedwell

The Latin name of common field speedwell is *Veronica persica*. It is also known as Buxbaum's speedwell, bird's eye, cat's eyes, cuckoo's leader and larger field speedwell. Other species of this plant are said to be good for healing wounds and clearing up respiratory complaints – hence the name speedwell. The name may also come from the fact that the flowers fall and blow away as soon as the plant is picked – hence speedwell, as in farewell or goodbye.

You can mount this design in a ready-made paperweight with a 3mm (¹/₈in) recess. However, I have used a glass shape that originally held an air freshener block bought in a supermarket.

You will need

- Basic equipment (page 8)
- Quilling papers:
- 2mm soft green for stems and sepals
- 3mm soft green for leaves and flower centres
- 3mm periwinkle blue and 3mm soft white for petals
- 3mm white for flower centres
- Glass shape
- All-purpose clear adhesive
- Tracing paper
- Prussian blue permanent marker

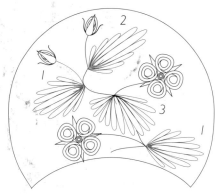

The pattern for the Speedwell quilling, shown full size.

Pin placements for leaf huskings.

Leaf 1: make two

Leaf 2: make one

Leaf 3: make one

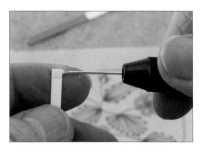

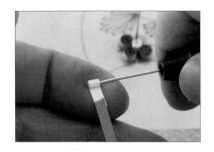

1 Stick 1.5cm (⁵⁄₈in) of a 3mm soft green strip to 2.5cm (1in) of a 3mm white strip and roll it from the green end to make a peg for the flower centre.

2 Photocopy the pattern and place it under the plastic of your quilling board. Make three closed loose coils from 5cm (2in) long, 3mm wide periwinkle blue strips. For the last petal, stick a 2cm (³⁄₄in) long, 3mm wide white strip to a 3cm (1³⁄₁₆in) long, 3mm wide blue strip. Roll another closed loose coil starting from the white end.

3 Lightly tint the white centre of the fourth petal using a Prussian blue marker pen before sticking it in place.

4 Glue two 2mm soft green strips in a cross shape on the back of the flower as shown.

5 When the glue has dried, turn the flower over and cut the strips into points to make sepals. Repeat steps 1–5 to make a second flower.

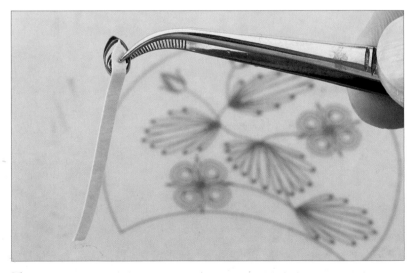

6 For the buds, make a closed loose coil using 5cm (2in) of a 3mm wide periwinkle blue strip. Press it into an oval shape. Make two buds.

7 To make the bud's front sepal, cut a length from a 2mm soft green strip, and cut the end into a point. Glue it to the bud as shown and then trim it to fit the length of the bud. Make one for each bud.

8 For the stem and the side sepals, take 1.5cm (⅝in) from a 3mm wide soft green strip. Snip into the end as shown, then separate the two snipped ends and use a cocktail stick to apply glue to their insides.

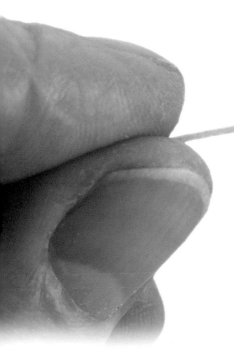

9 Stick the bud in between the glued ends as shown. Repeat steps 8 and 9 for the second bud.

10 Use 3mm wide soft green strips to make two leaf 1 huskings and one each of leaves 2 and 3 on the pattern on page 30. Make stems for the flowers and leaves using 2mm soft green strips, as in steps 22–24 on page 27 of the Lesser Celandine project. Place the air freshener glass shape on top of the pattern. Roll all-purpose glue on to the backs of the flowers and leaves and stick them down. Glue and position the buds and then trim the stems if necessary.

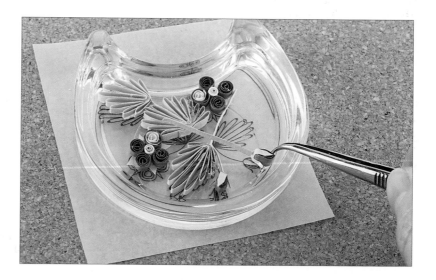

The finished Speedwell paperweight. If you recycle a glass air freshener that stands up on its own, as this one can, it also makes an unusual see-through ornament.

The Speedwell design has been worked vertically and a further flower added to create this pretty greetings card. (See template on page 184, top.)

Sweet Violet

The fragrance of sweet violet (Latin name *Viola odorata*) has been the scent of love for thousands of years. Greek mythology records it as the flower of Aphrodite, goddess of love. In medieval times the flowers were strewn on the floors of houses and churches to sweeten the air. Today oil distilled from its petals is used to make fragrances, toiletries and flavourings as well as a sweet liqueur, 'parfait amour'. The crystallised flowers are used to decorate cakes, puddings, ice creams and even salads.

The high brown fritillary butterfly lays its eggs on the stems and leaves of sweet violet and the caterpillars hatch in March or April and feed on the leaves. Artistic licence has been used in the pattern, as you will never see a high brown fritillary on a sweet violet in flower!

Choose a gift box to complement the colours of the quilling, or make your own. I have used a box made from lilac pearlised card.

You will need

- Basic equipment (page 8)
- Quilling papers:
- 3mm lilac for flower and bud
- 3mm yellow (also used on wings) and white for flower centre
- 3mm dusty rose for seed case
- 3mm mid green for leaves, sepals and stems
- 3mm saffron, gold-coloured, silver on ivory and silver on red for butterfly wings
- 3mm brown for butterfly body, legs, head and used in wings
- Gift box
- Craft foam pads
- Permanent markers: violet and pine
- Tracing paper

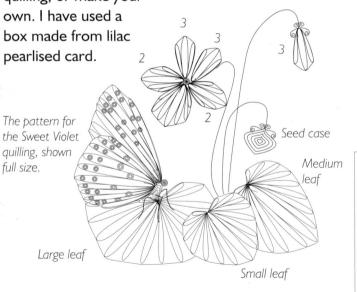

The pattern for the Sweet Violet quilling, shown full size.

Seed case

Medium leaf

Large leaf

Small leaf

Pin placements for petal and bud huskings.

2	2	2
I	I	I
Petal I	Petal 2	Petal 3 and bud

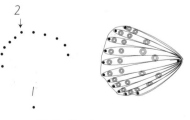

Butterfly's lower wing

Butterfly's upper wing

Pin placements and patterns for butterfly wing huskings.

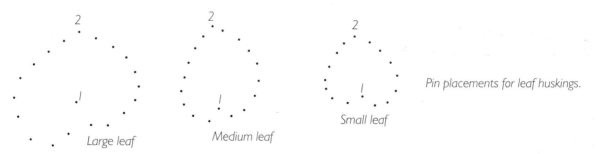

2 2 2

1 1 1

Large leaf Medium leaf Small leaf

Pin placements for leaf huskings.

1 Stick a 1cm (³/₈in) long, 3mm wide yellow strip to a 1.5cm (⁵/₈in) long, 3mm wide white strip. Place the yellow end in the needle tool at an angle as shown.

2 Roll the yellow strip. Place a dot of glue at the end of the yellow strip. Roll straight when you reach the glue. This makes a pistil for the flower centre.

3 Make one petal 1 husking, two for petal 2 and two for petal 3 (see page 36), using 3mm wide lilac strips. Glue them together with the centre as shown and touch up the edges with violet permanent marker.

4 Make a closed coil using 9cm (3½in) of a 3mm dusty rose strip. With the join at the top, pinch it into a diamond shape for a seed case.

5 Cut the end of a 3mm mid green strip as shown to make a stem and glue the tabs to the seed case.

6 Make two S shapes using 2cm (¾in) of a mid green strip. Glue one end of each to the stem and the other end to the seed case as shown.

7 Make another petal 3 for a violet bud and add a stem and S shapes in the same way as for the seed case.

8 Make collared huskings for the large, medium and small leaves (see page 37), using 3mm mid green strips.

9 Pin the large and medium leaves on to the pattern as shown, and use a cocktail stick to roll glue on to the surfaces where you will place the other leaf.

10 Place the third leaf on top of the first two as shown.

11 Use the pine permanent marker to give the impression of shade around the uppermost leaf.

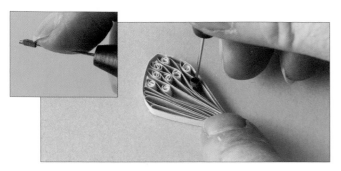

12 Make a collared husking for the butterfly's upper wing using 3mm saffron strips, following the diagrams on page 36. Then make open coils for the yellow markings using 1cm (3/8in) long, 3mm strips, and more open coils for the brown markings using 1.5cm (5/8in) long, 3mm strips. To place the markings, hold them on the needle with your fingernail and push them into the spaces in the husking as shown. You can hold the spaces open using tweezers.

13 Make the husking for the lower wing using 3mm gold-coloured strips, following the diagrams on page 36. Then make markings from open coils using 1cm (3/8in) long strips of silver on ivory and silver on red. Make some slightly larger markings using 1.5cm (5/8in) long silver on ivory strips. Place these as in the lower wing husking as before. To keep the markings in place, water down some PVA glue and use a cocktail stick to roll it over the surfaces of the wings.

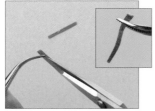

14 Make a closed coil for the butterfly's body using a 5cm (2in) long 3mm brown strip. Pinch it and turn one end up.

15 Cut slivers from a brown strip to make the butterfly's legs. Shape them using tweezers.

16 Pin the body to the quilling board as shown, place a tiny dot of glue on the leg and attach it to the body.

The butterfly's body with legs attached.

17 Pin the body in place on the pattern. Make a peg for the head from a 2cm (3/4in) long 3mm brown strip, and stick this on. Attach the upper wing.

18 Roll glue on to the edge of the upper wing using a cocktail stick.

19 Place the lower wing resting on the upper one. You will now need to unstick and carefully flatten out the box lid before proceeding.

20 Place the flattened box lid on the perforating mat and place the traced pattern on top. Use a pin to prick out the pattern on the box lid.

21 Glue the stems on the box lid. Glue the left-hand stem to the flower in two places to achieve the right shape.

22 Shape the seed case stem using your thumb.

23 Roll glue on to the backs of the leaves and stick them down.

24 Tuck all the ends of the stems under the central leaf.

25 Place a craft foam pad above the large leaf.

26 Peel off the backing and stick down the butterfly. Glue the ends of the feet and stick them down.

The finished Sweet Violet gift box.

A papier mâché box with recessed panels, painted to tone in with your design, makes a modern version of the wooden tea caddies that Regency ladies decorated with quilling. Here I have used different versions of the *Sweet Violet* pattern on each side of the box and on the lid (see page 187). A crochet strip stuck on the edges of each recess gives a nice finish to each panel.

Scarlet Pimpernel

The Latin name of this member of the primrose family is *Anagallis arvensis*. It is a creeping, low-growing plant with scarlet flowers (though they can be pink, white, lilac or blue), found on cultivated or disturbed ground. It was once thought to be a cure for madness and 'melancholy'.

Sir Percy Blakeney, the foppish hero of Baroness Orczy's novel *The Scarlet Pimpernel,* chose the name as his alias. The flowers open wide only in bright sunshine, making it difficult to spot at times, which is perhaps why it is associated with Sir Percy, known as 'that damned elusive Pimpernel'.

The flower's habit of opening only for a short time each day and closing during dull or wet weather has led to it being regarded for centuries as a combined barometer and clock.

You can make your own gift bag using metallic gold card, or buy one ready-made to decorate.

Bud

Half flower

Flower

Leaf

The pattern for the Scarlet Pimpernel quilling, shown full size.

The pattern for the ribbon slots and trims.

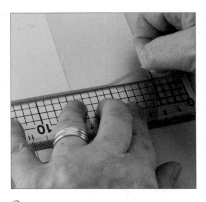

1 Open out the gift bag. Place a tracing of the ribbon slot pattern (page 42) over the top of the bag front. Use the ribbon slot punch, hammer and cutting mat to make ribbon slots 1.5cm (⁵⁄₈in) from the top.

2 Use a ruler to help you place a strip of 3mm (¹⁄₈in) wide double-sided tape 5mm (¹⁄₄in) from the bottom of the bag. Peel off the backing.

3 Place a 3mm crimson strip over the double-sided tape and stick it down, trimming the ends where required. Apply the trims at the top of the gift bag as indicated on the pattern on page 42.

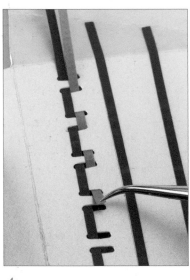

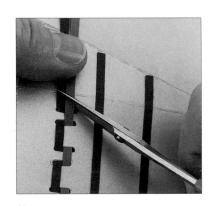

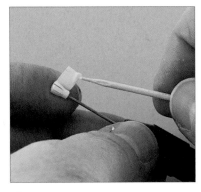

4 Use tweezers to thread 3mm crimson and green strips through the ribbon slots.

5 Trim the ends, cutting across both strips at an angle as shown.

6 To make a flower centre, take 4cm (1⁵⁄₈in) of 5mm ivory paper. Fringe it and roll it into a peg. Place a dab of glue on the end to close it.

7 To make a petal, use 4cm (1⁵⁄₈in) of 3mm crimson strip to make a closed coil and squeeze the end to make a teardrop shape. Make five petals.

8 Attach the flower centre to the quilling board with a pin. Glue the petals to the centre.

9 To make the sepals, take five short lengths of 3mm green strip and glue them to the back of the flower as shown.

10 When the glue is dry, trim the sepals to a point. Repeat steps 6–10 to make a second flower.

11 Make the calyx for the half flower from a 6cm (2³⁄₈in), 3mm wide green strip made into a closed coil. Press the coil into the handle of a needle tool to create a half moon shape.

12 Make closed coils for the three petals from 4cm (1⁵⁄₈in) lengths of 3mm crimson strip, shaped into teardrops.

13 Glue four 1cm (³⁄₈in) long, 3mm green strips to the back of the half flower for sepals, and trim them to points.

14 Make the bud calyx from a 6cm (2³⁄₈in), 3mm green strip made into a closed coil and shaped into a half moon using a cocktail stick.

15 Make the bud from a 4cm (1⁵⁄₈in) long, 3mm crimson strip made into a closed coil and shaped into a teardrop. Pin the calyx to the board and glue on the bud. Add two sepals in the same way as in step 13.

16 To make a leaf, make an eccentric coil (see page 14) from a 12cm (4³⁄₄in) long, 3mm green strip and shape it into a teardrop. Make six.

17 Place the pattern under the quilling board plastic and pin down the half flower. Make a stem from a 6cm (2³⁄₈in), 2mm green strip. Snip and glue the ends (see page 27) and stick the stem to the half flower.

18 Glue on the leaves.

19 Prick out the pattern on page 42 on the gift bag front. Stick on the half flower. Add a stem to the bud in the same way and stick it on.

20 Make stems for the main flowers as in step 17, push the tabs between two petals and glue the flowers to the bag. Trim the stems, add glue to the ends and push them into place using tweezers.

The finished Scarlet Pimpernel gift bag. I have added a bow attached by a craft foam pad and a ribbon handle threaded through holes punched with a hole punch. You can decorate the sides and back of the gift bag using varying combinations of the same flowers, buds, half flowers, leaves and stems as those shown in the steps.

A papier mâché box with a recessed and mirrored lid has been painted gold and flowers and half flowers from the Scarlet Pimpernel pattern adorn the recess. The mirrored centre has been edged with S-shaped scrolls and the edges of the lid and the bottom edges of the box have been decorated with red quilling strips. The template can be found on page 184.

Bluebells

This member of the lily family has the Latin name *Hyacinthoides non-scripta*. It lives in woodland, hedges and banks. The small white bulbs were used in the fourteenth century to make glue. The bulbs also contain starch which was used to stiffen the ruffs worn by the Elizabethan gentry.

Bluebells grow en masse in British woodlands, creating a wonderful display of brilliant blue. The flowers are fragrant and stand upright when in bud, but hang downwards when they are fully opened, nodding in the breeze. It is illegal to dig up wild bluebell bulbs for any purpose as we are in danger of losing this lovely flower.

You will need

- Basic equipment (see page 8)
- Quilling papers:
- 3mm (1/8in) cadet blue for the flowers, buds and bracts
- 3mm (1/8in) green for the stems and leaves
- Ready-made greetings card with blue border
- Pine green permanent marker pen

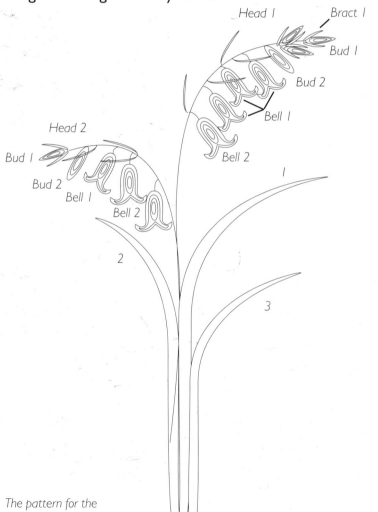

The pattern for the Bluebells quilling.

The pattern for the leaf wheatears.

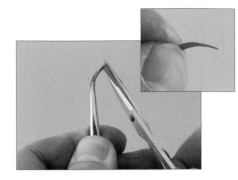

1 Take a 6cm length of 3mm cadet blue strip and roll it into a closed coil. Squeeze it into a teardrop shape to make bud 1 (see the pattern on page 48).

2 Pin the bud to the pattern on the quilling board and glue on a stem made from a 3mm green strip.

3 To make bract 1 (see page 48), take 1cm (3/8in) of a 3mm cadet blue strip, cut it into a triangle shape and curve it as shown using tweezers.

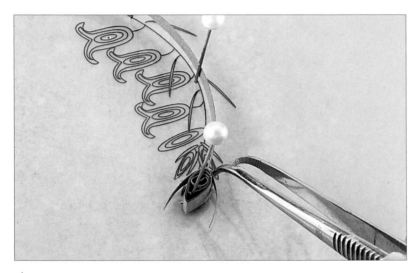

5 Make bud 2 using 8cm (3 1/8in) of a 3mm cadet blue strip, rolled into a closed coil and squeezed into a teardrop shape.

4 Make a second bract 1 in the same way and glue both to bud 1 as shown. Make two more of bud 1, complete with bracts, and attach them next to the first one as shown on the pattern.

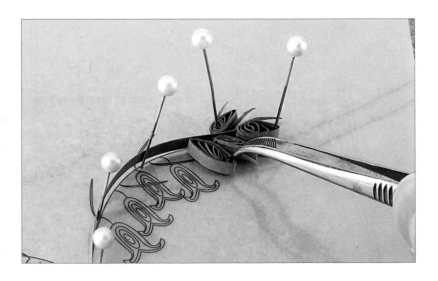

6 Place bud 2 as indicated on the pattern on page 48.

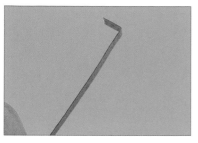

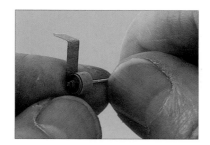

7 To make bell 1 (see the pattern), take a 12cm (4¾in) long 3mm cadet blue strip and bend back one end using tweezers.

8 Use the fine quilling tool to roll it from the other end.

9 Glue the end as shown to make a closed loose coil.

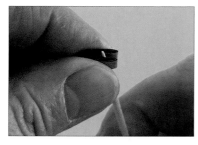

10 Squeeze the stalk end between your finger and thumb and shape the other end using a cocktail stick.

11 Shape the tips of the bell with your fingers.

12 Use tweezers to hold the bluebell and push the tips out with your finger and thumb.

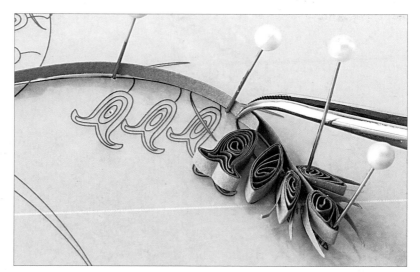

13 Curl the stalk back a little using a cocktail stick.

14 Glue the bluebell in place as shown.

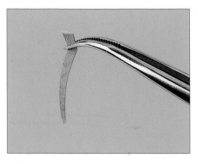

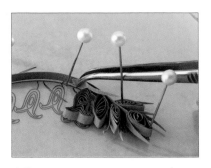

15 Cut and shape bract 2 in the same way as in step 3, using 2cm (¾in) of the 3mm cadet blue strip.

16 Glue and place the bract as shown using tweezers. It should reach over the tops of the bluebells.

17 Make and place another bract 2 on the other side of the stem.

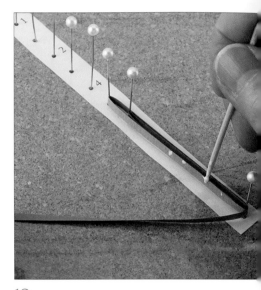

18 Continue making and placing the bells and bracts to complete head 1. Bell 2 is made in the same way as bell 1, but using a 15cm (6in) long strip. Complete head 2 in the same way, following the pattern on page 48.

19 Make wheatears for the leaves (see page 15), using the pattern on page 48 to show you the various lengths you need for the three leaves.

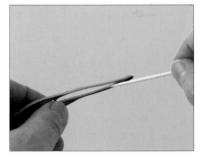

20 Apply glue inside the base of each wheatear to create the effect of a solid stem.

21 Pin the leaves on the pattern and glue the bases of the three wheatears together. Take them off when dry and use a cocktail stick to roll glue on the back of the base.

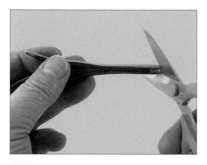

22 When the glue has dried, trim the ends of the wheatears to create a straight base.

23 Place the pattern on the card and prick it out with a pin to mark the placing of the various components.

24 Apply glue where the main stem and leaves will go and stick them down. Roll glue on to the backs of the flowers using a cocktail stick and adhere them in place on the card. Apply glue in the same manner to the backs of the flowers and stick them in place. The ends of the flower stems are tucked between leaves 1 and 2 and secured with glue.

25 Use the pine green marker to darken the main stem, to cover any unevenness caused by handling the paper.

The finished Bluebells greetings card.

This memo board will bring a breath of spring into your kitchen. I painted a ready-made blank MDF whiteboard to tone with the quilled design of bluebells and lesser celandines. I then stuck a piece of card behind the shaped top aperture and added the quilling. The pattern can be found at the top of page 186.

Three-Dimensional Quilling
Making Characters

by Jane Jenkins

I wonder how many quillers remember that rolls of wallpaper used to come with an extra blank strip at the edges, which had to be cut off with a pair of scissors before the pasting could begin. None of you is old enough, I'm sure! But I remember playing with these cut-off coils of paper, rolling them tightly and pushing them into shapes.

A couple of decades later, I remembered that fun when teaching history to eight-year-olds. We were 'doing' the Vikings and needed horns for our papier-mâché helmets. I, like everyone else at the time, was unaware that there is little historical evidence for horned helmets so we happily rolled up wide strips of paper and pushed them into cone shapes which made great horns, to the delight of the children.

Another decade later, I began making models with quilling and realised, once again, the value of cone coils, cup coils, solid coils and ring coils. With them, we can create fabulous quilled characters, simple and fantastic, human and animal, serious and comical. Cup and cone coils can be found often in antique quilling but not for making characters so we modern quillers can proudly say we are breaking new ground, using old techniques and making history.

Three-dimensional quilling is such a joy – everyone should try it, so I hope this chapter will provide help and inspiration for those who need it.

Materials

Quilling strips

Quilling strips come in a large variety of colours and types. The standard length is 45cm (18in). The standard width is 3mm but three-dimensional quilled characters often make use of wider strips – between 5mm and 15mm is normal.

The perfect weight paper for quilling strips is around 100gsm. However, paper manufacturers sometimes make lovely colours, but in the wrong weight for quilling, so that they feel softer or stiffer than is usual. This is not much of a problem, mostly, but the size of tight coils – the coils we use most in model making – can be considerably affected by these differences. Strip lengths or numbers, therefore, might not always be given because it is more helpful for you to know the final diameter required.

Antique quilling often made use of strips with a gilt edge. As usual, modern quillers have taken this old idea, developed and modernised it and make use of strips with not only metallic gold foil but also silver, holofoil, pearlised and more – wonderful for fairies' wings. Some strips also are made from super-shiny 'mirror' paper, not so easy to work with but the results are well worth it (see the Angel project on page 92).

Paper sheets

Sometimes it is more convenient to use strips that you have cut by hand from sheets of paper. The angel's hands require small rectangles of coloured paper and the Poodle project (page 76) uses tubes made from wider strips. Take care that the paper you cut is the same white as the pre-cut quilling strips.

Glue

The best glue for most quilling is PVA. Good quality PVA is pure white – not transparent in any way until it is allowed to dry. It also has a thick, creamy consistency and is suitably tacky. Use as little as possible; a good quiller produces work with absolutely no glue marks. You will also need extra strong PVA glue for less absorbent papers, like the gold mirror strips used for the Angel project.

Other equipment

Cocktail sticks These can be used not only for applying glue, but also as a tiny dowel to form a long, thin cone.

Kebab stick This is used as a dowel when something slightly wider than a cocktail stick is required.

Wooden dowels I have these made specially in my favourite sizes but you can get sets of them from suppliers.

Quilling tools Personally, I prefer not to use a tool for normal rolling because there is a danger of producing coils with a bent-back middle. However, there are some occasions when this would not show and a tool can be very helpful.

Tweezers I find these invaluable and have different ones for different jobs but the projects in this chapter simply need one easy-to-hold, fine or extra-fine pair.

Scissors If you are cutting your own wide strips for pom-poms, tubes etc., a long pair of scissors is useful. Then you will need a very fine, straight pair for fringing and general fine work.

Onion holders and masking tape For spreuer-work, when you make the wings for the Angel project on page 92.

Ruler To measure strip widths and tight coil diameters.

Fine fibre-tip black pen For marking in eyes.

Dowels of various sizes and shapes To help make ring coils.

Clockwise from top left: masking tape, kebab stick and cocktail sticks, wooden dowels, quilling tools, fine and extra-fine tweezers, long and fine scissors, onion holders, a ruler, pencil, fine fibre-tip black pen and various dowels.

Basic techniques

Closed loose coil

Closed loose coils may be formed into a variety of shapes. This is how I make the basic coil using a half-length 3mm strip.

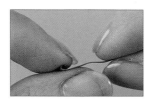

1 Scratch the tip of the strip with your fingernail against your thumb to curl it.

2 Bend over the very tip of the strip. It can help to have slightly damp fingertips.

3 Rub your finger along your thumb and the strip will begin to roll between them.

4 Continue rolling to the end of the strip, then release the coil. It will spring open.

5 Glue down the end of the coil where it naturally lies. Do not pull it into place.

Closed loose coils can be squeezed into many different shapes, as shown.

End-to-end rolling

This is achieved by gluing two strips together end-to-end before rolling, to create a coil with a different colour towards its centre.

Solid coil

This is simply a coil rolled as tightly as possible and glued down. A perfect solid coil has a smooth, even surface and no hole at its centre. A fine, smooth coating of PVA glue can help. Instructions often do not give strip length or numbers because you simply roll, adding more strips as necessary, until the coil reaches the given diameter.

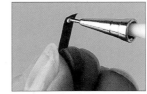

1 Scratch the end of the strip a great deal, until it is quite soft.

2 Roll the end, aiming to leave no hole at the centre.

3 Roll the strip tightly. Do not release it. Glue the end.

A selection of solid coils.

Cup coil

These are made from solid coils. Some quillings need quite deep cup coils and two glued together can make a 'ball'.

1 Press the solid coil into a dome shape.

2 To prevent the coil from collapsing, use your finger to coat the surface of the cup coil with glue.

To make an oval solid coil, fold the beginning of the strip instead of rolling. An oval cup coil can be made by pushing the oval solid coil into a dome shape.

A selection of cup coils. With oval cup coils, you may have to push glue into the centre as well as across the surface, and squeeze as it dries, to ensure a good, secure coil.

Cone coil

Cone coils are also made from solid coils but usually with wider strips. Cone coils may be tall and thin or big and wide. The trick is to achieve this size and shape without the coil collapsing! I call my favourite method the 'Marycooze method', named after the lady who invented it.

Marycooze method

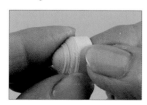 

1 Use three 5mm wide strips to make a solid coil. Push it into a cup coil to get it started.

2 Hold the coil between fingers and thumbs and press it with alternate hands. The cone grows like magic!

Dowel method

You can push the cone into shape using a wooden dowel, which can be bought in sets or made specially.

Potter's method

Turn the cone on your finger and shape it by pressing your finger and thumb together as you turn.

A selection of cone coils. There is nothing worse for a quiller than achieving a super, tall, smooth cup or cone coil, only to have it collapse or break, so all of them must be coated with a fine layer of PVA glue. I usually use my fingers for this, rather than a brush, because that way I can sense any weaknesses. Coat either the inside or the outside, or both surfaces of your coil. The outside is more messy, but will give good protection against marks and dust.

You can push a cone coil into a curved shape or press it into an oval while the inside coating of PVA is still wet.

Ring coils and tubes

These can be made around dowels of various diameters from a cocktail stick to a mixing bowl. You can even make your own dowels to the required size, using card. I prefer to start coils on a dowel and then slide them off and continue by hand. A ring coil made from a very wide strip might more accurately be called a 'tube'.

Various dowels used to create ring coils. Coat the face of ring coils with glue as with cup and cone coils.

A selection of tube coils, made using wide strips.

Wheatears

This is how to make the basic wheatear. It can then be formed into different shapes.

1 Make a loop at the end of a strip and glue it in place.

2 Bring the strip around the first loop to make a slightly larger loop.

3 Hold the loop sideways while you put a tiny dot of glue at the pointed end. Bring the loop round again and repeat.

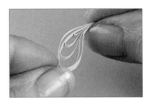

4 Continue to loop until the wheatear is as big as you want it to be, adding more strip if necessary. Finally, glue down the end.

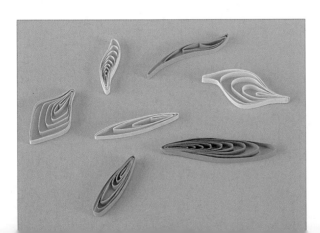

A selection of wheatear coils.

Pom-poms

These are made by rolling a fringed length of paper, usually a wider than average strip. Fringing is quicker if the paper is folded first.

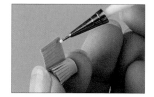

1 Take a half-length 10mm wide strip and fold it in half twice. Fringe it up to 3mm (¹/₈in) from the edge.

2 Unfold the fringed strip, roll it up and glue down the end.

3 Spread the fringes.

A selection of pom-poms. Pom-poms can be made in different sizes by altering the lengths and widths of strips.

Tendrils

These are useful for characters' arms and legs.

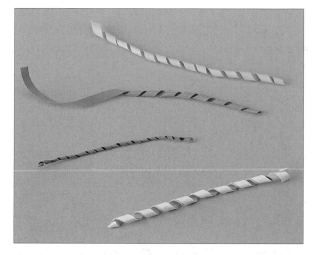

1 Roll a 3mm wide strip 'helter-skelter-like' along a cocktail stick or other dowel.

2 Take the tendril off the dowel and then stretch and twist it to tighten it.

A selection of tendrils.

Finger Puppet

The very first quilled models I made were finger puppets; they are very simple, small but not too fiddly and, of course, there is plenty of scope for variation. Children love them too, both to make and to play with, since they are really quite strong, especially if coils are all coated with PVA glue. Once you have got the idea, the possibilities for making more to join the gang are endless but if you should get short of ideas, just ask a child to come up with more.

You will need

Four 5mm white strips
One 5mm bright pink strip
Four 5mm peach/flesh-coloured strips
One 5mm yellow strip
One 5mm pink strip
One 5mm black strip
Fine black fibre-tip pen
Kebab stick
Dowel

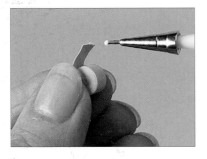

1 To make the head, roll a peach/flesh-coloured strip as tightly as possible with little or no hole at the centre. Glue down the end.

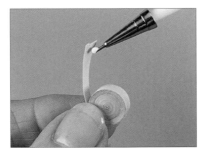

2 Add another strip and continue to roll. Glue down the end to make a solid coil.

3 To make the mouth, glue ⅛ of a pink strip to ⅛ of a black strip and roll them up, beginning at the black end. Release the coil completely and glue down the end.

4 Push this closed loose coil around the curve of the solid coil and glue it in place.

5 Add a third peach/flesh-coloured strip and roll as tightly as possible. Add a fourth strip and roll tightly.

6 Glue down the end of the fourth strip to complete the face.

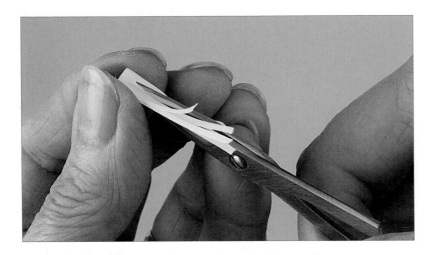

7 To make the hair, fold a 6cm (2³/₈in) long 5mm wide yellow strip in half and snip as finely as possible up to an eighth of the fold.

8 Glue to the head, off-centre, to give the finger puppet a side parting. Repeat with a 4cm (1⁵/₈in) long strip at the other side and then give her a haircut if necessary.

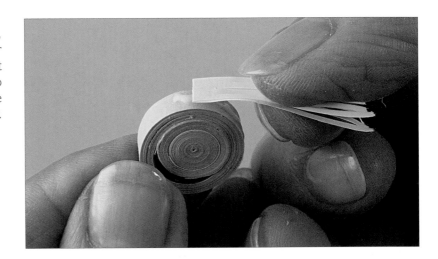

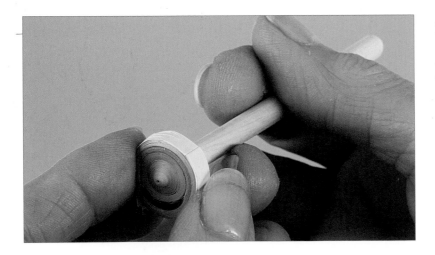

9 Push a dowel into the centre back of the head to make a nose appear at the front. Coat the back of the head with glue so that it remains firm.

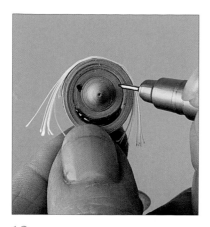

10 Mark the eyes with a fine black fibre-tip pen.

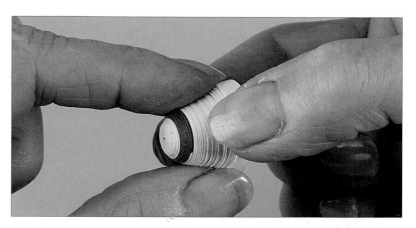

11 To make the body, roll up a white strip as tightly as possible. Glue it down, add first a bright pink strip and then three more white strips to make a solid coil. Shape into a cone coil, around 3cm (1¼in) tall.

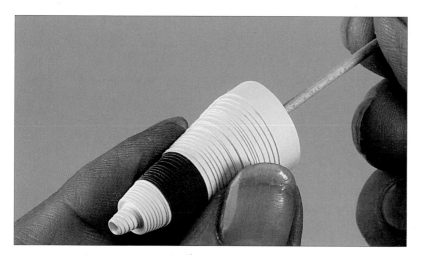

12 Use the flat end of a kebab stick to create a neck by pushing up the centre of the coil and then coat the whole body with PVA glue.

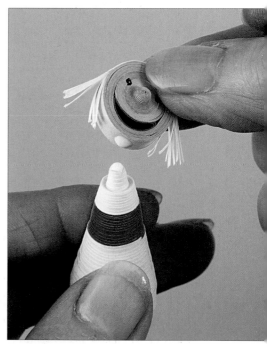

13 To glue the head to the body, put a blob of glue on the neck and another on the head and wait for them to go tacky before sticking them to each other.

Opposite

The finger puppet characters in this happy scene can be made using the items shown at the bottom left of this page.

The earrings are ring coils formed around a pencil or smaller dowel. Use a quarter-length strip, preferably 2mm wide, but 3mm will work.

The spectacles are ring coils formed around a pencil or smaller dowel. Use a quarter-length 2mm wide strip if you can. Then make a thick strip with four 1cm (³/₈in) lengths glued together. Bend this and link the rings together.

The ears and mouth are closed loose coils made from eighths, or even sixteenths, of a 2mm or 3mm wide strip. Form them into ear or mouth shapes.

The long hair is made by snipping 5mm wide strips (see step 7). Curve them a little and glue to the head, backwards. Give the puppet a haircut if necessary. For the fringes, snip very short 5mm wide strips. Curve a little and glue to the head, forwards. Trim the fringe if necessary. Hair can be made curly by rolling the ends a little before gluing to the head.

Long-legged Frog

I got the idea for these long-legged characters when I saw some wooden ones with string arms and legs. They are happiest sitting around looking cute but you could also make them into simple puppets by fixing strong thread or shearing elastic to the head. Arms and legs will lollop around to the great amusement of all.

You will need

Approximately twelve 10mm wide dark green strips

Approximately twenty-five 3mm wide dark green strips

Fifteen 3mm wide light green strips

Three 3mm wide black strips

One 3mm wide white strip

Cocktail stick

PVA glue

Fine scissors

15mm (⅝in) dowel

1 To make the body, use about eight 10mm wide dark green strips to make a cone coil approximately 4.5cm (1¾in) tall.

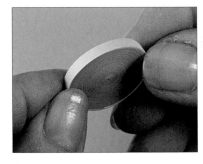

2 To make the head, use 3mm wide dark green strips to make a solid coil. Continue adding strips, one at a time, until the coil is 2.25cm (⅞in) in diameter. Add an extra light green strip to define the mouth.

3 Press this solid coil into a cup coil and coat the inside with glue. Before the glue is dry, press the coil into an oval shape.

4 You need to make two of these coils. Glue them to each other so that the mouth is a little open. Put a blob of glue on the outside rim of the top coil and on the inside rim of the bottom coil and wait for the glue to go tacky before pressing the coils together.

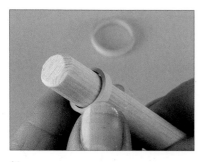

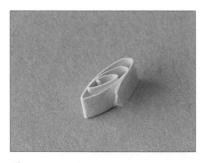

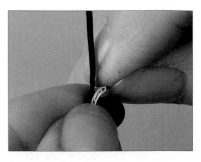

5 To make the eyes, wrap a 3mm wide, full-length, light green strip around a pencil to make a ring coil. Glue down the end. Make another, larger ring about 2cm (¾in) in diameter.

6 Roll a 3mm wide, 2cm (¾in) long, white strip. Release it and press it flat.

7 Roll a black 3mm wide strip into a solid coil. Do not roll the whole black strip. When about 8cm (3¼in) is left, incorporate the tiny white coil and continue rolling the black. Glue down the end. This will make an eye with that all-important highlight.

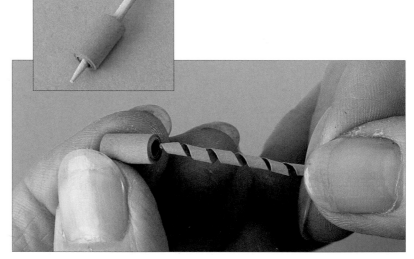

8 Make a larger eye with a highlight, this time using two black strips. Glue each black eye inside a green ring coil and glue them both to the frog's head.

9 To make the arms and legs, use 3mm wide strips, quarter length for the arms and a third length for the legs. Make them into tendrils and push each end into a ring coil (tube) made from a quarter of a 10mm wide strip, rolled around a cocktail stick.

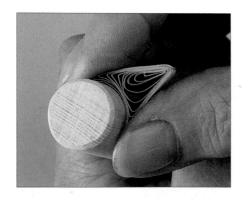

10 To make the hands and feet, use 3mm wide strips to make twelve wheatear coils. Each of the three wheatears needed for a foot will use up as much of a full-length strip as possible. Cut off any excess strip. Each wheatear for the hands uses about a half-length strip. Shape each wheatear using a 15mm (⅝in) diameter dowel as shown.

11 Glue three shaped wheatears to each other.

12 Glue the hands to the arms and the feet to the legs.

13 Glue the arms to the shoulders. Glue the legs to the inside of the body as shown.

The finished Long-legged Frog project.

This relaxed-looking bird is the same as the frog with the following exceptions: the head is a 'ball' made from two cup coils, each using six 5mm wide strips. The beak is a curved cone coil made from one 5mm wide strip. The neck is a ring coil (tube) made from a 4cm wide, 6cm long strip, rolled around a kebab stick. Eyes with highlights are made from half-length black strips. The head tuft is an eighth of a 5mm wide strip, cut as finely as possible and curved.
The wing is made from three wheatears.

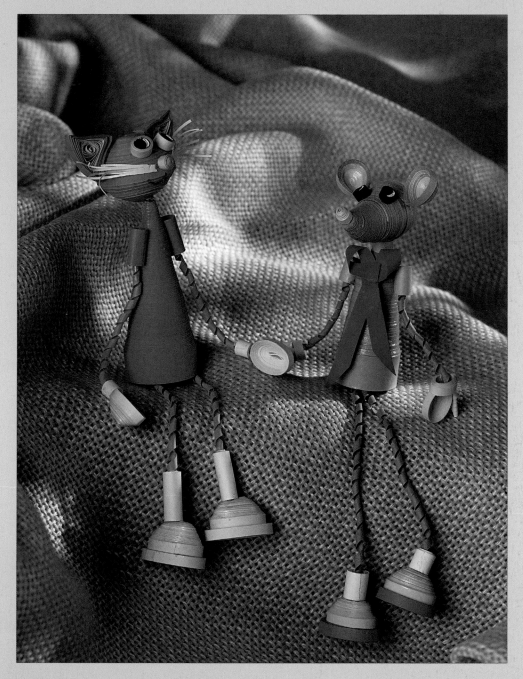

The cat's head has the same coils as the frog but they are glued together and closed to make a flattened ball. The hand is an oval cup coil made from a full-length strip. The shoes are oval solid coils made from two and a half 3mm wide strips, glued to an oval cup coil of two 3mm wide strips. The ears are closed loose coils, half a peach/flesh-coloured strip glued to a half orange strip, 'end-to-end' rolled; roll from the peach/flesh end and press into a triangle shape. The eyes are solid coils made using a quarter-length black strip with an eighth green strip added.

The mouse's body, arms and legs are as for the frog. The back of the head is a cup coil made with six 3mm wide strips. The front of the head is a curved cone coil of six 5mm wide strips. Push to 3cm (1¼in) in length and then curve slightly. The nose is a cup coil made from a quarter-length, 3mm wide strip. Ears are a cup coil of two 3mm wide strips, shaped. The eyes are as for the frog, using half-length black strips. The neck is a quarter-length ring coil using a 10mm wide strip. The hands are oval cup coils, each made from two full-length strips. Their thumbs are cone coils made from a quarter-length, 5mm wide strip, using a cocktail stick as a dowel. The shoes are as for the cat.

Poodle

A very small version of this poodle appeared in my book, *Quilling Techniques and Inspiration*. I have had lots of requests for instructions so here they are, for a slightly bigger, less fiddly version. You can always adjust the sizes of the strips to make smaller ones, if you like. This poodle requires a few exceptionally wide strips. You could cut these yourself from sheets of plain paper, which can be bought from a good supplier.

1 To make the head, first take three 5mm wide white strips to make a curved cone coil which should be 2.5cm (1in) long.

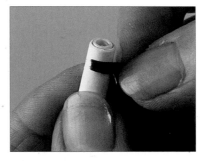

2 Then use three 3mm wide strips to make a cup coil. Glue it to the curved cone coil.

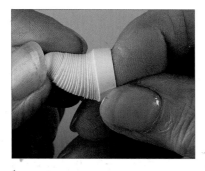

3 To make the nose, use a quarter of a 3mm wide pink strip to make a tiny cup coil. Glue it in position.

4 To make the neck, roll a 15mm wide white strip until it has a diameter of 7mm (¼in). Tear off any excess strip and glue down the end. To make the collar, wrap half a 3mm wide scarlet strip around the neck, 2mm (¹⁄₁₂in) from the top.

5 To make the medallion, use half a 2mm wide deep yellow strip to make a solid coil. Glue this to the neck, just below the collar.

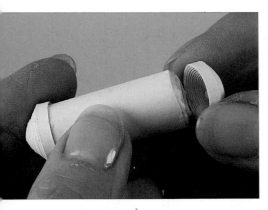

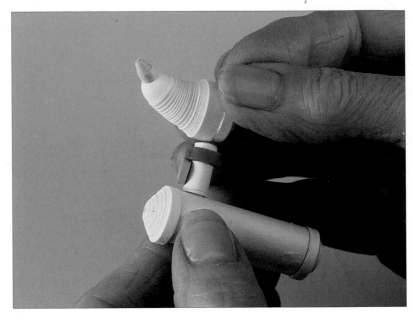

6 To make the body, roll enough 3.5cm wide white strips around a pencil to make a ring coil (tube) 15mm (⁵⁄₈in) in diameter. Use 3mm wide white strips to make a cup coil of the same diameter and glue this over the end of the tube. Make another for the other end.

7 Glue the head, neck and body together.

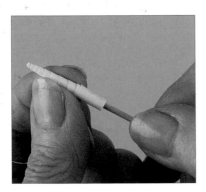

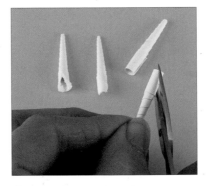

8 To make the tail, use a quarter of a 10mm wide white strip to make a tall, thin cone coil, 3.5cm (1³⁄₈in) long. A cocktail stick makes a good dowel and is also good to ensure that the inside of the tail is well coated with glue. Glue the tail on to the body.

9 Make four legs in the same way and cut the top of each diagonally so that they will better fit the curve of the body.

10 Finely fringe an 8mm wide white strip. Divide it into four. Glue one fringed piece to the pointed end of a leg and wrap it around as tightly as possible. Glue down the end. Coat the base of the foot with glue.

11 Spread out the fringes as far as possible. Do this to all four legs and then glue them to the body.

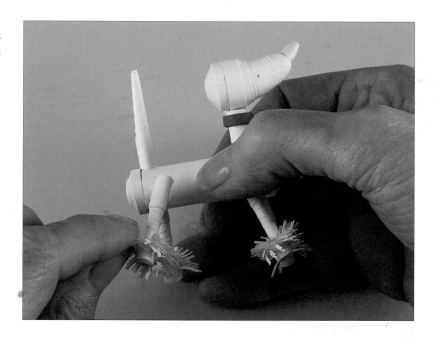

12 To make the ears, fringe a 10mm wide white strip and tear it into quarters. Make a pom-pom out of each and glue two to each side of the head.

13 Make two more of these pom-poms, exactly the same, and glue them either side of the tail tip.

14 Fringe a 10mm wide full-length white strip and make it into a pom-pom to be placed at the dog's shoulder. You need one for each side.

15 Make two smaller pom-poms in the same way for the dog's hips, this time using half-length strips.

16 Fringe a half-length, 15mm wide strip and roll it up tightly. Glue this to the top of the poodle's head and then spread out the fringes a little.

17 Finally, use a very fine fibre-tip pen to draw in the poodle's eyes.

Opposite

The finished Poodle project. The bowl is a solid coil made from 3mm wide strips, 2.5cm (1in) in diameter, with a ring coil placed around its edge. The bone requires four cup coils, each made from a 3mm wide, full-length strip, making two 'balls'; and a tube made around a cocktail stick from a quarter-length, 10mm wide strip.

You can make balls of various sizes and colours by gluing two cup coils together. The little rug is made from an oval solid coil using lots of 10mm wide fringed strips; just keep on fringing and adding until the rug reaches the right size or you are exhausted! If you alter the leg positions, you can make poodles that crouch or sit.

Our pampered pink friend above has a dog basket made from 5mm wide strips. I used six to make a strong ring coil, 6.5cm (2½in) in diameter, and filled it with closed loose coils. The sides of the basket are also made from closed loose coils, mainly using half-length strips and shaped into eye shapes.

Fairy Figure

One of the problems with a free-standing three-dimensional quilling is how to make sure it stands up. I found it especially challenging with this fairy, whose wings tended to make her fall over backwards. I solved the problem by strengthening and enlarging the wings so that she actually stands by balancing on the tip of one wing as well as on her feet. Solving problems such as this is part of the joy of quilling characters – nothing is impossible, it is just a question of trial and error, and a lot of time! I am pleased with this final result, especially with the very modern, holofoil-edged strips which make her glisten with silvery colour.

1 To make the bodice, use one 5mm wide lilac strip to make a cone coil. Press it into a slightly oval shape.

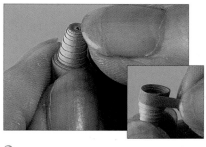

2 Flatten the pointed end so that the fairy's waist will not be too narrow. The final height should be 15mm (⅝in). Add a quarter-length, 3mm wide mauve strip.

3 For the skirt, use five 5mm wide lilac strips to make a cone coil, not too pointed at the waist (height 3cm; 1¼in). Add a quarter-length mauve strip to the coil. Coat the inside with PVA and before it is dry, flatten the coil a little.

4 To make the shoulders, use one 3mm wide peach/flesh-coloured strip to make a shallow cup coil. Press this into an oval to fit inside the bodice.

5 To make the neck/choker, use an eighth of a 2mm wide mauve strip to make a tiny ring coil around a cocktail stick. Glue it on to the shoulders.

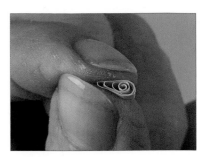

6 To make a sleeve, use a full-length 3mm wide mauve strip to make a fairly deep cup coil. Flatten it a little before the glue coating dries. Make two.

7 To make the arms, use a quarter of a 5mm wide peach/flesh-coloured strip to make a long, thin cone coil. A cocktail stick makes a good dowel. Push the point back so that the wrists are not too narrow. The final length should be about 15mm (⅝in).

8 To make the hands, use an eighth of a 2mm wide strip to make a closed loose coil. Shape it into a teardrop.

9 Glue the sleeve, arm and hand to each other using tweezers to help you and then glue the whole thing to the bodice. Remember that two blobs of glue, if left to go tacky, will stick together instantly.

10 Make the legs and feet in the same way as the arms and hands but use a half length for each leg and an eighth of a 3mm wide strip for each foot. Legs should be 3cm (1¼in) in length. Glue them to the inside edges of the skirt.

11 Glue the bodice section to the skirt.

12 To make the head, use two 3mm wide peach/flesh-coloured strips to make a shallow cup coil. Repeat, using pale yellow, and glue the coils together to make a ball.

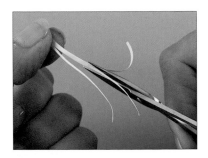

13 For the hair, cut nine eighth lengths of 3mm strips in pale and canary yellow. Fringe them lengthways as finely as possible, up to 3mm (¹⁄₈in) from the end.

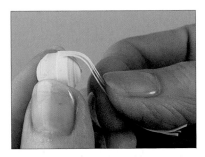

14 Curve into gentle 'S' shapes and glue three to the head, where it meets the face.

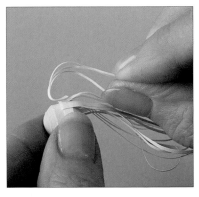

15 Curl one end of six more fringed lengths right over as shown and glue them to the edge of the face.

16 To make the upper wings, use holofoil-edged silver-coated 3mm wide strips to make nine wheatear coils which have only three loops at their rounded ends. The smallest should be approximately 2.5cm (1in) long. Make them very slightly bigger each time so that the longest is 5.5cm (2¹⁄₄in) long.

17 Glue these to each other and put a tiny dot of glue on the rounded end of each. Glue on another strip at the wing base and wrap it around the wheatears to hold them all together. Carry on wrapping round to use up as much strip as possible but finish it at the base of the wing. Glue down the end.

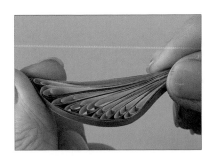

18 Give the wing a pinch at its top to make a good wing shape.

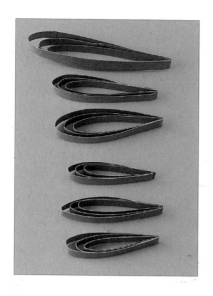

19 To make the lower wing, use 3mm wide, holofoil-edged mauve strips to make six wheatear coils with only three loops at the rounded ends. One wheatear should be 4.5cm (1¾in) long; two should be 4cm (1⅝in) long and three should be 3cm (1¼in) long.

20 Glue them to each other in this order: small, medium, small, long, medium, small.

21 Put a tiny dot of glue on the rounded end of each wheatear. Add another strip to the base and wrap it snugly around all the wheatears. Use as much of the strip as possible. Cut off any excess.

22 Make a tiny solid coil from a quarter-length, 3mm wide mauve, holofoil-edged strip and glue it to the tip of the wing.

23 Glue a silver-coated, holofoil-edged strip to the base of the wing and loop it around to enclose the tiny solid coil within the wing. Pinch into a pointed shape.

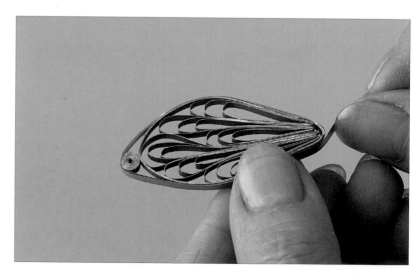

24 Glue the upper wing to the lower wing and then to the back of your fairy.

25 Make a second set of upper and lower wings and glue them to the other side of the fairy's back.

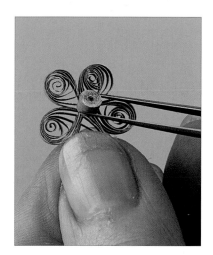

26 To make the decorative flower for her dress, use five 2mm wide, eighth-length strips for petals. Make each into a closed loose coil teardrop shape. The flower centre is a tiny solid coil made from a sixteenth of a 2mm wide strip.

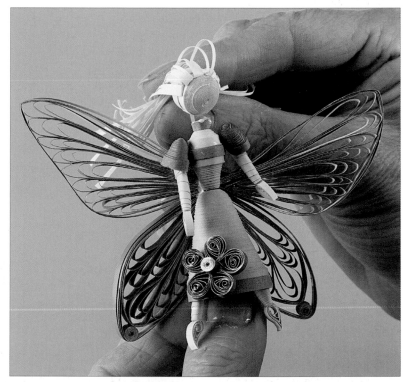

27 Finally, glue on the fairy's head.

The finished Fairy Figure with woodland friends!

The elves: the head, neck, sleeves, face, arms, feet and hands are as for the fairy. The legs are as for the fairy but shorter. The knees are a shallow cup coil made from a quarter of a 2mm wide strip. The body is a 2.5cm (1in) tall cone coil made from three 5mm wide strips. The thumb is a closed loose coil made from a sixteenth of 2mm wide strip. The wings are made from three wheatears (as for the fairy but smaller), glued to each other with no enclosing loop.

The flower hat has six petals: closed loose coil teardrops made from quarter-length, 2mm wide strips. The six sepals are closed loose coil long, thin teardrops made from eighth-length, 2mm wide strips. The stalk is a cone coil made from an eighth of a 5mm wide strip.

The toadstool cap is a cup coil made from 3mm wide strips to a diameter of 3.5cm (1³⁄₈in). The toadstool stalk is a cone coil made from 5mm wide strips to a diameter of 2cm (³⁄₄in) and then pushed to a height of about 2cm (³⁄₄in). Toadstools can be made in a huge variety of shapes by altering these lengths.

Fairies and an elf in different colours gather in the woods.

Angel

Here, the challenge is to make a large figure. The cone coil that makes her tunic is 10cm (4in) tall and has to be carefully worked using the potter's method (see page 61) so that it very gradually grows to the required size. The angel's wings are made using a technique which is not strictly quilling but derived from Swiss straw-work. Instead of a coil, you produce a 'spreuer' (rhymes with soya) which is made on a comb or, in this case, two onion holders. If you choose to make the wings from the very shiny mirror paper strips, you will need to use a stronger PVA glue.

You will need

White strips: approximately forty 15mm wide and twelve 10mm wide

Peach/flesh-coloured strips: approximately fifteen 3mm wide; two 5mm wide and one 1.5mm wide

Strips in various yellows: approximately fifteen 3mm wide; six 5mm wide and four 2mm wide

Two 3mm wide white gold-edged strips

Four 2 x 3cm (¾ x 1¼in) peach/flesh-coloured paper rectangles

Approximately thirty-five 3mm wide bright yellow gold-edged strips

Approximately twenty 3mm wide mirror strips, gold surface

Two onion holders, masking tape and a pencil

Very fine black fibre-tip pen

Tweezers

Cocktail stick

PVA and extra-strong PVA glue

1 To make the angel's body, use 15mm wide white strips to make a solid coil, 5cm (2in) in diameter. Work this into a cone coil, 10cm (4in) tall and coat it with PVA glue.

2 For the collar, roll a quarter-length, 10mm wide white strip around a pencil to make a ring coil. Cut it diagonally as shown. Glue it to the body.

3 To make the head, use 3mm wide peach/flesh-coloured strips to make a cup coil, 3cm (1¼in) in diameter. Repeat, using any yellow strips randomly. Glue the two cup coils together to make a ball.

4 For the nose, use an eighth of a 1.5mm or 2mm wide strip to make a tiny cup coil. Coat the inside with glue and position it on the face.

5 Draw in the eyes using a very fine black pen.

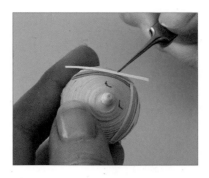

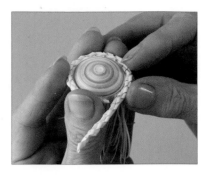

6 To make the hair, cut six 5mm wide yellow strips into quarters and fringe each lengthways as finely as possible, up to 3mm (⅛in) from the end. Glue these along the back of the hair/face join line.

7 Cut some 2mm wide strips in shades of yellow into 3cm (1¼in) long lengths. Glue to the centre of the forehead and back towards the ear position. Use yellows randomly and overlap occasional ones.

8 To make the wreath, use three half-length white 3mm wide gold-edged strips to make tendrils. Twist them together and glue the wreath around the hair/face join. Cut off any excess.

9 For the sleeves, use 10mm wide white strips to make a solid coil, 2cm (¾in) in diameter. Shape into a curved cone coil, approximately 5cm tall.

10 Coat the inside of each coil with glue and before it dries, press it into an oval shape.

11 To make the fingers, use 5mm wide peach/flesh-coloured strips. Each finger is a tiny cone coil made from an eighth of a strip and pushed on to a cocktail stick.

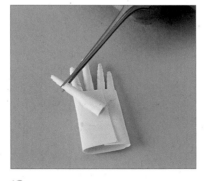

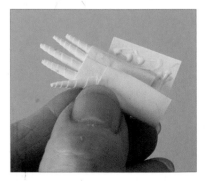

12 Glue four fingers together. Use a 2 x 3cm (¾ x 1¼in) strip to wrap around the base of the fingers to make a hand.

13 Use tweezers to place the thumb coil on the hand a little lower than the fingers.

14 Wrap another 2 x 3cm (¾ x 1¼in) strip around the hand to enclose the thumb. Make a second hand.

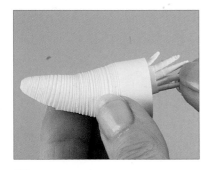

15 Glue each hand inside a sleeve with the thumb uppermost.

16 Glue on the sleeves and the head. Remember that two blobs of glue, if left to go tacky, will stick together instantly.

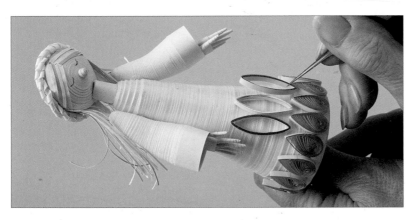

17 To make the decoration on the tunic, use 3mm wide bright yellow, gold-edged strips. Along the hem are closed loose coils shaped into teardrops, each one made from a full-length strip. Above them are ring coils (also one strip) made around a 15mm (1 1/8in) diameter dowel and pressed into eye shapes. Glue the decorations on as shown.

18 Fix two onion holders together, side-by-side, using masking tape and a pencil to hold them rigid. Mark prongs 14, 19 and 25.

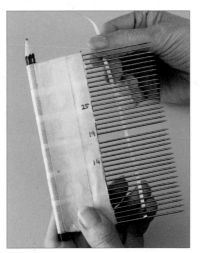

19 To make the angel's wings, use 3mm wide mirror strips to create large spreuers. Make a tiny loop at the end of a strip and glue it firmly. Slot this loop on to the bottom prong of the onion holders and take it up the back as shown.

20 Loop the strip over prong 26 and bring it down to the base again.

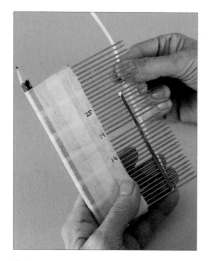

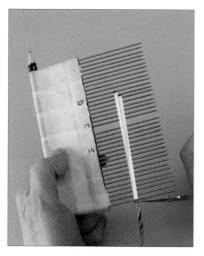

21 Put a tiny dot of glue at the base and then bring the strip up behind the onion holder again.

22 Go over prong 25 on the right, then back down to the base and glue the strip in place. The strip is running out, so trim the end and stick on another strip. This is how to add more strips whenever you run out.

23 Take the new strip up and over prong 24 on the left, then down to the base. Glue it.

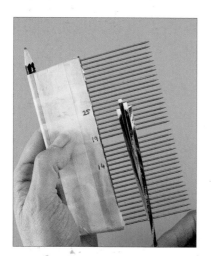

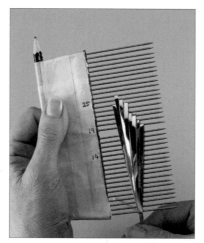

24 Go over prong 24 on the right, down to the base and glue.

25 In the same way, go over prongs 23, 22, 21, 20 and 19 on the right side only. Always glue at the base.

26 Take the strip over prong 19 on the left, down to the base and glue.

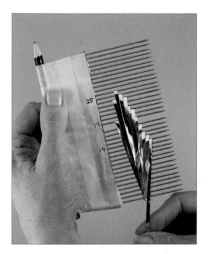

27 Now go over prongs 18, 17, 16, 15 and 14 on the right only. Glue at the base.

28 Take the strip over prong 14 on the left, down to the base and glue.

29 Now go over prongs 13, 12, 11, 10, 9, 8, 7, 6, 5, 4, 3 and 2 on the right only.

30 When the glue is dry, slide the spreuer off the onion holders.

31 Repeat to make a second wing and glue them both to the angel's back, using extra strong PVA glue. Remember that two blobs of glue, left to go tacky, will adhere instantly.

The finished Angel project. Having done a little 'angel research', I find that haloes are optional! If you want yours to have one, use a 3mm wide gold mirror strip to make a ring coil about 3cm (1¼in) in diameter and glue it to the back of the angel's head.

This angel's lacy overskirt was made on a former, slightly bigger than the angel's tunic. I made the former from soft modelling clay covered with plastic food wrap. The closed loose coils, ring coils etc. were glued to each other and held in place with pins until the glue dried. When complete, the overskirt could be slipped off the former and attached to the tunic.

Miniature Quilling

by Diane Boden Crane

One of the things I like most about the craft of quilling is that it can be practised using a range of paper widths, depending on the effect you want to achieve. Although I first learnt the craft using paper strips 3mm wide (there was very little 2mm paper available at the time), I soon had the desire to create more delicate designs using finer strips. One answer was to cut 3mm strips in half down the centre, but as time went on, 2mm strips became much more readily available. Today, we are spoilt for choice when it comes to the colour and finish of narrow strips. No longer is 2mm-wide paper the Cinderella of the quilling world!

Stationery and an aperture frame decorated with quilled autumn leaves (see page 114).

Through this chapter, I hope to inspire readers with designs that concentrate on fine quilling. Some parts still call for 3mm-wide paper of course, but 2mm, 1mm, 1.5mm and occasionally 0.5mm-wide strips have also been used. The technique of spiralling features quite heavily in some of the projects. It is an ideal use of very narrow paper and adds a different texture and dimension that contrasts well with more traditional quilled shapes. However, many of the familiar basic shapes have still been used and there is much that will be familiar to the seasoned quiller.

I have tried to illustrate a number of applications for miniature quilling, from conventional greetings cards and photograph frames to napkin rings and a selection of quilled chocolates that look good enough to eat!

In my experience as a quilling teacher, students seldom look back once they have experienced the satisfaction of working with narrow paper strips. Even though the difference may be only a millimetre, the results appear much more delicate and pleasing to the eye. One phrase I have heard repeatedly over the years has been, 'I never knew quilling could be this small'! It is my hope that I can give quillers the confidence to experiment with narrow strips to produce miniature quilling of which they can be proud.

These quilled chocolates look good enough to eat (see page 126).

Materials

The chief requirements for miniature quilling are paper strips, a quilling tool, scissors and glue. You can add to these basic items as you go along.

Paper strips

Quilling strips come in packs that have been pre-cut to size and can be bought in a variety of different widths. This chapter uses paper 2mm and 3mm wide, although sometimes these strips are cut down to 1mm wide (for example for spiralling), 1.5mm and occasionally 0.5mm wide (for example for decorating the chocolates). The papers are easier to work with if they are encouraged out of their figure-of-eight formation. This can be achieved by laying them flat in a shallow tray or box.

A standard British quilling strip is approximately 450mm (17¾in) in length. You should find that papers 2mm wide are readily available through quilling suppliers and it is possible to order paper that is 1mm wide. However, often it is more convenient and economical to simply cut the paper to the required width yourself. This may seem a daunting task at first, but like everything else, patience brings its own reward!

Occasionally, I have used pearlised and metallic strips that have a treated edge. This effect becomes more pronounced once the paper has been coiled or wound.

Equipment

Various **quilling tools** are available commercially, and the finer the tool the better, especially when it comes to miniature quilling. Try to find a tool that has a fine slit. **PVA glue** is the most widely used glue and is ideal for the job. Try to use very small amounts – you will find a **fine-tip applicator** an enormous help. It dispenses a tiny dot of glue and is controlled by a gentle squeeze of the bottle. **Cocktail sticks** are invaluable when picking up very small pieces of quilling. Alternatively, some people prefer using **fine tweezers**. A pair of good-quality **scissors** is an essential part of your equipment. Make sure the blades have short, sharp points to give you an accurate cut. For making spirals, I generally use **rose wire**. This is a fine wire that needs to be handled with care as it bends easily. You will need an ordinary metric **ruler** for measuring the lengths of your strips, and a metal one for cutting card etc.

Other useful items include a **pair of compasses**, a **2H pencil** (this gives a good sharp line) and a **craft knife**. Cutting on a **self-healing mat** saves your blade and the surface of the dining room table! **Round-headed pins** in different sizes are ideal when making a dome out of a solid coil, and **chalk pastels** are great for backgrounds – they come in a wide range of colours and are very economical to use.

Papers and cards

It is a good idea to collect a selection of papers, cards, etc. to set off your quilling. Several projects use a plain box as a base – you might be lucky and find the exact colour you want, or you may end up having to cover the box with paper. I found saved foil wrappers very useful when it came to the quilled chocolates (see pages 126–131)! For the project on page 120, I used a blank card frame, obtainable from good craft stores.

Tissue paper is a handy addition to the quiller's store, as it rolls up beautifully when making paper sticks.

Basic techniques

If you look closely at a paper strip you will notice that the two sides are different. The 'right' side looks and feels smooth at the edges where the paper turns down very slightly. Consequently, the 'wrong' side of the paper appears rough at the edges. Try to get into the habit of always rolling the paper with the smooth side on the outside of your coil, as this will make your quilling look more even. Although this chapter is about miniature quilling, do not be tempted to roll the paper too tightly! The paper lengths may be quite short in some cases, but there still needs to be a certain amount of 'give' in the coil to enable you to make a well-defined shape.

If you are new to quilling, practise rolling with 3mm-wide strips to begin with, before attempting to quill with finer strips.

A basic coil

The secret of good quilling is to keep an even tension as you roll the paper strip. This will produce a more regular, evenly spaced coil.

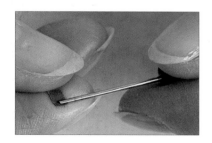

1 Line up the end of the paper strip on the quilling tool.

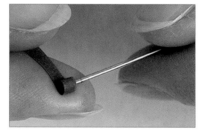

2 Turn the tool so that the paper winds tightly around it.

3 Release the coil.

4 Put a dot of PVA glue on the end of the strip. Try to use as little glue as possible for a neat finish.

5 Seal the coil by pressing down firmly on the seam using a cocktail stick.

A finished basic coil.

Basic shapes

All of the shapes shown below are used in the projects in this chapter. They are all made from a basic coil.

Teardrop
Pinch the coil into a point using your thumb and forefinger.

Eye shape
Pinch the coil at both ends using using your thumbs and forefingers.

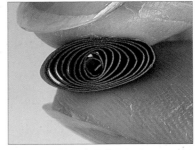

Oval
Gently squeeze the coil between your thumb and forefinger, with the join on one side.

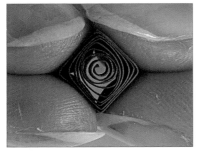

Square
Make an eye shape, then pinch the other two sides to form a square.

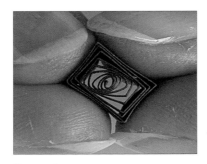

Rectangle
Make in the same way as a square, but with two long sides and two short sides.

Leaf shape
Make an eye shape, then gently press two opposite edges together.

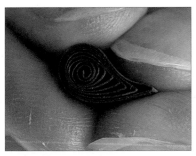

Petal shape
Pinch the coil into a teardrop, pulling the point over to one side.

Heart shape
Make a teardrop, then put a dent in the rounded end using your thumbnail. Alternatively, use the point of a cocktail stick.

Tip
When making shapes, always pinch your coil at the glued join to help hide it.

Peg

As the peg is made of solid paper, it is worth taking the trouble to smooth out the layers and tidy the centre, which will improve its appearance.

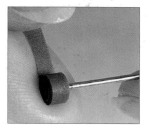

1 Roll a tight coil, but do not let it go.

2 Glue the end of the paper strip, keeping the coil tight, while it is still on the tool. Remove the tool and tap the peg down to even out the layers.

3 Place a cocktail stick in the centre of the peg and twist it to make the centre smooth.

A finished peg.

A solid coil

This is not an easy technique to master but is well worth the effort. The coil is formed using the fingers only, without the use of a quilling tool, to avoid forming a hole in the centre. Try to keep the coil very tight as you roll, and do not let go too soon!

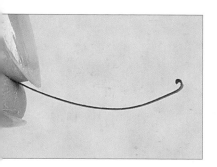

1 Turn over the end of the paper strip as tightly as possible.

2 Roll the strip by hand into a tight coil.

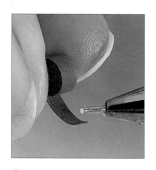

3 Apply a dot of PVA glue to the end of the strip, keeping the coil tight.

A finished solid coil.

Spiral

Spiralling takes practice to achieve a uniform result. As with rolling coils, the secret is in maintaining the tension – holding the paper taut while rotating the wire. Spirals work well using 1mm- or 1.5mm-wide strips.

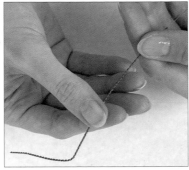

Tip
Cut a 2mm strip down to 1mm by eye, using a sharp pair of scissors.

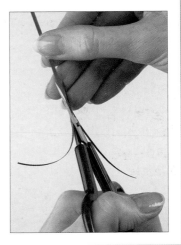

1 Dampen the end of a 1mm paper strip and wind it on to a piece of thin wire at a 45° angle. Hold the paper and twist the wire, not the other way round.

2 When you have wound on the whole strip, carefully remove the wire by pushing the paper off the end.

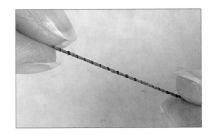

3 Tighten up the spiral by pulling and twisting it at the same time.

Paper sticks

The important things to remember when rolling paper sticks are to roll around the wire as closely as possible and to roll centrally, keeping the ends even.

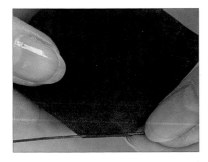

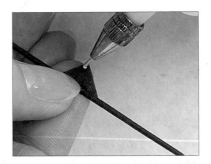

1 Fold the corner of a small sheet of tissue paper over a length of thin wire and glue it down using PVA.

2 Roll the tissue paper tightly around the wire.

3 Glue the end of the paper in place and remove the wire.

Daisies and Lavender

This simple floral design is used here to create a greetings card. It combines two different ways of using an aperture. A thick card template is used to make a sturdy paper frame to support the lavender, and the daisies are attached to a lattice background, which has been created with double-thickness paper strips.

The open space behind the quilling really shows off the beauty of the craft, which can sometimes be lost when the quilling is simply glued to a solid background. Care must be taken to ensure that the quilling touches the inside of the frame at various points so that it is well supported.

You will need

Lavender sprigs, 3mm strips
Thirty-six mauve strips,
45mm (1¾in) long

One pale green strip,
450mm (18in) long

Four pale green strips,
225mm (9in) long

Daisies, 2mm strips
Forty-two white strips,
75mm (3in) long

Six yellow strips,
75mm (3in) long

Twelve mid-green strips,
56mm (2¼in) long

Raised frames, 3mm strips
Three mid-green strips,
450mm (18in) long

Lattice windows, 2mm strips
Seven pale green strips,
450mm (18in) long

Two mid-green strips,
450mm (18in) long

Other materials
Five small pieces of cardboard,
44 x 25mm (1¾ x 1in), for
frame template

White card, 210 x 150mm
(8¼ x 6in), scored in half
to make a card blank 210 x
75mm (8¼ x 3in)

Mauve card, 205 x 70mm
(8 x 2¾in)

Pale green paper, 205 x
145mm (8 x 5¾in),
for insert

1 Photocopy the template below at 200 per cent, and copy it on to mauve card. Glue the mauve card on to one side of the white card using PVA glue. Working on a cutting mat, cut out the apertures using a craft knife and metal ruler.

2 For the lattice windows, glue two 2mm pale green strips together using PVA glue. Work on one 50mm (2in) section at a time.

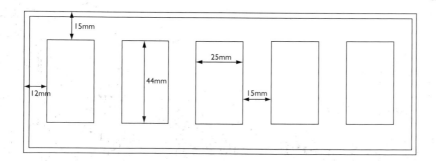

15mm

44mm

25mm

12mm

15mm

Template for the card, half actual size.

108

3 Stick the two strips together by holding them at the sides between your thumb and forefinger, and pulling the paper through. Do this for each of the seven pale green strips, cutting the seventh strip in half and gluing the two halves together.

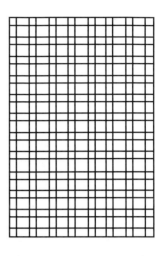

Template for the grid, used to align the paper strips in step 4 below. Reproduced actual size.

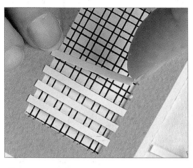

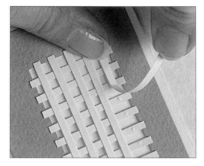

4 Cut the double-thickness strips into eight 28mm (1¼in) strips and five 47mm (1¾in) strips for each lattice window. Place the grid behind the aperture and use it to position the horizontal strips accurately. Glue them in place using a small dab of PVA glue applied to the card at each end.

5 Attach the vertical strips in the same way, applying glue to the card at each end and to the horizontals to secure them.

6 Frame each lattice window using the 2mm mid-green strips. Glue on the verticals first, then the horizontals. Apply the glue to the card, lay on the green strip then cut the strip to the correct length.

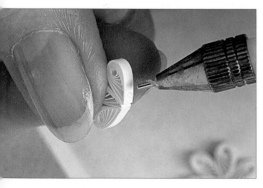

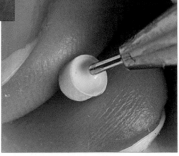

8 For the centre of each daisy, make a yellow peg and dome it by pushing up the centre using the round end of a pin. Seal the inside with PVA glue.

7 For each daisy, make seven white teardrops and glue them together in a circle.

  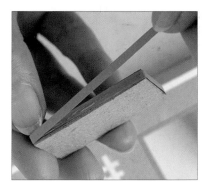

9 Glue a yellow peg to the centre of each daisy, then attach two daisies to each lattice. Apply the glue to the back of the daisies, not to the lattice. Make four mid-green eye shapes for the leaves and attach two to each daisy using the end of a cocktail stick.

10 Build the raised frames for the remaining two windows around a 3mm (1/4in) thick block, the same size as the apertures, made by gluing together layers of cardboard.

11 Wrap a 3mm mid-green strip around the block four times. Apply glue in between each layer. Attach a 450mm (18in) strip first, then continue with a second strip to complete the frame. Cut off the end of the second strip.

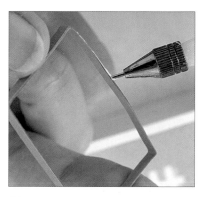  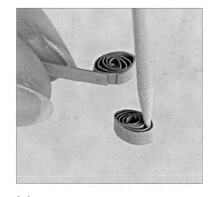

12 Remove the frame from the block, and apply glue along the lower edge.

13 Attach the frame to the card.

14 For the lavender stems, cut the 450mm (18in) pale green strip into two equal lengths and glue them together to make a double-thickness strip (see step 3). For each sprig, cut a 45mm (1¾in) long stem from the double-thickness strip and make nine mauve ovals for the flowers. Attach two flowers at the top of the stem.

15 Work down the stem in pairs, always applying the glue to the stem and not to the flowers.

16 Complete the sprig by gluing the ninth flower between the pair at the top.

  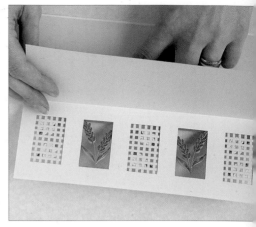

17 Fit one lavender in the frame, gluing it at the points where it touches the frame. Fit in the second, smaller, sprig, trimming the stem to size.

18 Finally, make four pale green leaf shapes and attach one leaf shape to each lavender sprig, postioning the leaves using a cocktail stick.

19 Fold the pale green paper in half to form an insert, and glue it in place along the top inner edge of the card.

The completed card.

The frame and lattice techniques described in the project can be used on their own to good effect. The greetings card uses pegs in between the frames to support the design. Both the box and the card feature a single lavender stem, suspended by a thin spiral of paper. The basic technique has been adapted further to create place settings.

Autumn Leaves

Every autumn I marvel at the variety of colours and shapes of the falling leaves. This design uses just a few leaf patterns, but these can be created in a number of autumnal colours to make an interesting design.

The leaves would look good glued to a plain wooden box, or alternatively you could use a card box that has been covered in brown parcel paper first, similar to the one shown here. The acorn and oak leaf gift tag continues the theme.

This design is worked entirely in 2mm-wide paper strips in a range of browns, reds and yellows.

Oak leaf

1 Make six small petal shapes, and glue two together at the pointed end so they curve outwards. Make a small teardrop and glue it between them to form the top of the leaf.

2 Attach two more pairs of petal shapes. For the base, make an oval, then put a dent in one side and wrap it round the end of the leaf.

The completed oak leaf.

You will need

Box

Oak leaf
Eight strips, 56mm (2¼in) long

Sycamore, horse chestnut and maple leaves
For each larger leaf:
Three strips, 150mm (6in) long
Two strips, 112mm (4½in) long
Two strips, 56mm (2¼in) long
Small double-thickness strip for stem
For each smaller leaf:
One strip, 112mm (4½in) long
Four strips, 75mm (3in) long
Small double-thickness strip for stem

Ivy leaf
One strip, 150mm (6in) long

Ash, elder and rowan leaves
For each larger leaf:
Seven strips, 75mm (3in) long
Small double-thickness strip for stem
For each smaller leaf:
Five strips, 75mm (3in) or 56mm (2¼in) long
Small double-thickness strip for stem

Other materials
Circular blank box, 115mm (4½in) diameter

Tag

Leaves
Five brown strips, 150mm (6in) long

Acorns nuts
Three pale green strips, 150mm (6in) long

Acorn cups
Three brown strips, 180mm (7in) long

Stems
Double-thickness brown strip
70mm (2¾in) long (trim to size)

Other materials
Pale brown chalk pastel

Soft tissue paper

Circular white card, 60mm (2¼in) diameter, with a hole punched through at the top
One red 2mm strip, 450mm (18in) long

Sycamore, horse chestnut and maple leaves

The range of leaves I have created in this group are shown opposite. They consist of seven or five eye or leaf shapes arranged in a circle, with a stem made from a short, double thickness paper strip at the base. The shapes can either all be the same size or vary, with the largest at the top of the leaf, and the smallest at its base. The instructions below are for the larger leaf shown top left, but can easily be adapted to suit which ever leaf type you choose to make.

1 Glue three large eye shapes together to form the top of the leaf, then glue two medium-sized eye shapes below these.

2 Attach the two small eye shapes at the bottom to complete the leaf.

3 Apply glue to the inside edges of the lower two leaves and insert the stem.

Ivy leaf

1 Start with an oval, and pinch the top to make three points.

2 Pinch the other end in the same way to form a total of five points.

3 Alternatively, form the other end into a single, curved point, as you would for a petal shape.

Ash, elder and rowan leaves

These leaves, shown opposite, consist of two or three pairs of eye or leaf shapes arranged down a stem, with a single shape at the top. As before, the stems are made from a short, double-thickness strip. The instructions below are for a larger leaf, like the one shown top left, but can easily be adapted to suit which ever leaf type you choose to make.

Apply glue to the stem, and position the shapes using a cocktail stick. Allow each shape or pair of shapes to dry before moving on to the next.

Decorating the box

Make a selection of leaf shapes in a variety of sizes and colours, and arrange them in an S-shaped pattern on the box lid. Make some single leaf and eye shapes as well to fill in any gaps in your design. Position the shapes first, then glue them all down when you are happy with your arrangement.

The tag

1 For each of the five leaves, start with an oval and pinch it at both ends to form six points.

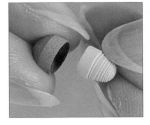

2 Make the acorns from two solid, domed coils. Make the cup slightly wider using a longer paper strip so that the nut fits inside it comfortably. Glue the nut inside the cup.

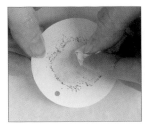

3 Colour the centre of the tag using pale brown chalk pastel applied with a piece of crumpled soft tissue paper.

4 Make two stems, 25mm (1in) long, from double thickness strips and glue them to the card along their thin edge.

5 Glue on the acorns and leaves. Complete the tag by threading a spiral made from a 1mm red paper strip (cut from a 2mm strip; see page 107) through the hole.

The completed box and tag.

The leaf sections on the napkin rings have been edged individually with gold- or copper-edged quilling strips. The leaves have been made following the same methods as in the project, before being arranged and glued to the rings.

The napkin rings have been made from sections of card tube – the type found in the centre of a kitchen roll. They have been covered with a decorative paper and trimmed with paper strips in brown and gold.

In the picture below, a selection of different-coloured leaves have been used to decorate stationery. The leaves on the greetings card have been carefully arranged around the aperture before being glued down. The background has been first coloured using chalk pastels (see page 120). This card could also be used as a photograph frame.

Butterflies

The subject of butterflies continues to be a popular choice for those who enjoy quilling. Their wings can be made in a number of different ways, but I have chosen to quill them using conventional shapes with a 'paper bead' for the body section.

Limiting the number of colours used brings simplicity to the design and it is interesting to note how the colours appear different depending on the order in which they are used. Originally, the butterflies were flying around on the photograph frame, but they looked a little lost. I later decided to add leaves and stems to the background, which gave them something to 'sit' on and drew the design together. Sometimes, leaving a design for a while and coming back to it at a later stage allows you to view it differently and so make improvements to it.

You will need to make seven butterflies all together for this project; make each one using different-coloured paper strips for the wings.

1 Sprinkle the larger sheet of pale green paper with shavings from a yellow chalk pastel. Blend in the colour using a piece of crumpled soft tissue paper, then apply green chalk pastel.

2 Blend in the green pastel.

You will need

For one butterfly

Top wings, 2mm strips
Two pale yellow strips, 45mm (1¾in) long
Two purple strips, 75mm (3in) long
Two mauve strips, 75mm (3in) long
Two pale yellow strips, 112mm (4½in) long

Lower wings, 2mm strips
Two mauve strips, 75mm (3in) long
Two purple strips, 112mm (4½in) long
Two pale yellow strips, 112mm (4½in) long

Body
Rectangle of brown parcel paper, 80 x 10mm (3¼ x ⅜in) cut down to a point at one end to make a long, narrow triangle

Antennae, 1mm strips:
One brown strip, 30mm (1¼in) long

Leaves and stems

Leaves, 2mm strips
Twelve green strips, 112mm (4½in) long
Stems, 1.5mm strips
Three green strips, 450mm (18in) long

Other materials and equipment

One green 1.5mm strip, 450mm (18in) long
One yellow 1.5mm strip, 450mm (18in) long
Blank oval frame, 170 x 130mm (6¾ x 5in)
Pale green paper, 190 x 150mm (7½ x 6in), to cover front of frame
Pale green paper, 170 x 130mm (6¾ x 5in) to cover back of frame
Yellow and green chalk pastels
Soft tissue paper
Long pin

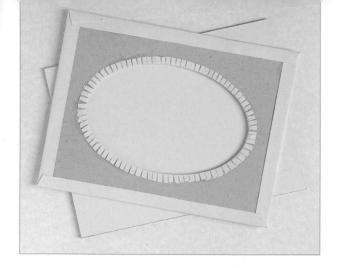

3 Use the coloured paper to cover the front of the frame. Cut off the corners of the paper and fold the edges of the paper behind the frame. Glue them in place. Cut out the aperture, leaving a 10mm (⅜in) border. Snip into the border, fold it behind the aperture and glue it in place. Cover the back of the frame using the other sheet of pale green paper.

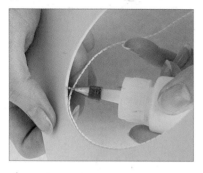

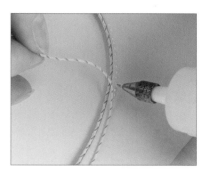

4 Make a spiral from a 1.5mm yellow strip. Apply glue to the lower edge of the inside of the frame and attach the spiral. Work in 50mm (2in) sections.

5 Make a spiral from a 1.5mm green strip, and attach this to the inside of the frame above the yellow spiral. Apply glue to both the yellow spiral and the edge of the frame to secure it.

6 Make a full length green spiral, and attach it to the frame to form the main stems. Start at the top of the frame on the left, then take the spiral round the base of the aperture and up the right-hand side. The right- and left-hand sides should be mirror images of each other. Apply the glue to the frame, not to the spiral, and work in 50mm (2in) sections.

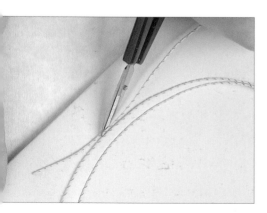

7 Make the other stems and attach them in the same way, cutting the spirals to the correct length after they have been glued to the frame.

The completed stems.

8 Make twelve leaf shapes and attach them to the frame. Apply the glue to the backs of leaves and position them using a cocktail stick.

9 For the upper wings, glue
together a purple and a mauve
strip, and roll up the strip into
a coil. Unwind the coil until the
centre is large enough to hold
a peg.

10 Place a pale yellow peg
made from the 45mm (1¾in)
long paper strip in the centre of
the coil using a cocktail stick.

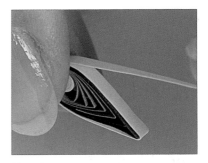

11 Make the coil into a
teardrop, and wrap the 112mm
(4½in) pale yellow strip around
the outside. Join it on at the tip
of the teardrop, wrap it around
three times, glue down the end
and cut off the excess.

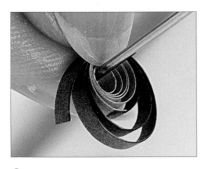

12 For the lower wings, make
a mauve teardrop, then wrap
around it three times with a
purple strip, then again with a
yellow strip. Make two pairs of
wings, each consisting of an upper
and a lower wing glued together
at their tips. Glue the two pairs of
wings together.

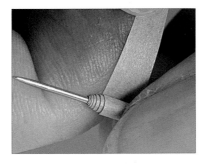

13 For the butterflies' bodies,
coil the triangular piece of brown
parcel paper around a long pin,
starting at the base of the triangle.
Glue down the end and remove
the pin.

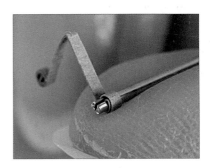

14 For the antennae, fold the
30mm (1¼in) length of 1mm
brown paper strip in half and
make a coil at each end. Seal
each coil with glue.

15 Glue the antennae into the end of the body, and glue the body to the wings, applying the glue to the wings and then laying the body on top.

16 Make seven butterflies using different-coloured strips and glue them to the frame.

The completed frame.

The delicate nature of butterflies lends itself perfectly to glassware. The butterflies and leaves on the glass vase shown on the left have been made using pearlised paper, which gives them a beautiful sheen. They have been attached to the vase using small squares of double-sided sticky tape.

Spiralling comes into its own in the greetings card shown below. A length of spiral has been threaded through a series of pegs to create an open framework on which to rest the butterflies. For the smaller butterflies, simply halve the measurements.

At the other end of the scale, the box shown below has been decorated with butterflies twice the size of those made in the project. Spiralling has been used to complete the design.

Chocolates

This project is great fun to work on as it provides a good deal of scope to use your imagination once the basic chocolate shapes have been mastered. I have found it very useful to keep the identification charts from boxes of chocolates to provide further inspiration. Not every subject translates well into quilling, but these chocolates work wonderfully well, and really do look 'edible'! I have seen many people do a double take when looking at them for the first time.

The colour of the paper strips is an important factor, so try to use strips that resemble chocolate as closely as possible. As purple is such a popular choice for chocolate packaging, I have chosen to use it as the base for the chocolate box, and in different shades for the variations.

Basic chocolate shapes

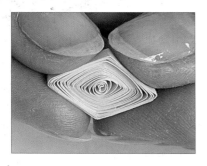

Diamond
Make two squares, pinch each of them into a diamond shape and glue one on top of the other.

Oval
Make two ovals, dome the centre of one of them and seal it with glue, then glue the two ovals together.

Rectangle
Make five small rectangles and glue them together, one on top of the other, to form a block.

Circle
Make two solid coils and slightly dome one of them. Glue the two coils together.

Dome
Make a solid coil and dome the centre. Apply glue inside to prevent it collapsing.

Decorating your chocolates

Chocolate sprinkles
1 Make a spiral from a 1mm strip, cut it into 50mm (2in) strips and snip off tiny lengths on to a piece of scrap card.

2 Cover the top surface of your chocolate shape in glue and roll it in the sprinkles. Decorate the sides of the chocolate in the same way, once the top has dried.

Icing strips
Make a spiral from a 0.5mm paper strip, attach it at one end underneath the chocolate, then wrap it around several times. Glue the spiral underneath when you have finished and snip off the excess.

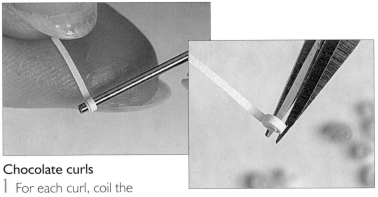

Chocolate curls
1 For each curl, coil the end of a 1mm strip three or four times around a quilling tool.

2 Cut off the curl.

The finished chocolates

Cover a diamond shape in white chocolate sprinkles and glue a 1mm spiral to the top as shown. Make two pegs from 20mm (¾in), 1mm-wide strips and glue them to the ends.

Cover a dome shape in chocolate sprinkles, make a 1mm spiral and glue it down in a series of loops.

Make a white chocolate dome, then cut 0.5mm strips and glue them across the chocolate. Edge the base with a 1mm-wide strip.

Start with a rectangle and decorate it with a 1mm spiral. Glue it underneath the chocolate at one end and wind round, securing with glue at various intervals.

Cover an oval shape in a square of foil. Fold the excess foil underneath and trim to neaten if necessary.

Cover an oval shape in chocolate sprinkles and decorate it with icing strips (see page 128).

Make a square chocolate and glue a 0.5mm spiral over the top as shown.

Cover a square shape in white chocolate curls, and decorate it with icing strips (see page 128).

Wind and glue a 1mm spiral around a dome-shaped chocolate, starting at the top. Make an 'almond' from a 1mm strip, 112mm (4½in) long, formed into a teardrop.

Make a circle shape using white chocolate-coloured paper. Snip tiny pieces from a 1mm-wide strip, dot glue over the top of the chocolate then sprinkle them on. Glue a 2mm-wide strip around the base.

The final arrangement of chocolates on the lid.

The finished chocolate box. I have made a selection of different chocolates and scattered these around the base to show you the endless variations that are possible.

This arrangement of chocolates in a box frame has a fun, contemporary feel. The background of squares was made using a square stencil cut from a piece of card. I drew faint lines on the backing as a guide, then rubbed on two different shades of purple chalk pastel, a square at a time, using crumpled soft tissue paper.

The chocolate gift bag and matching tag shown below would be an appropriate choice for a chocoholic. Just don't forget to put some real chocolates inside the bag!

Fairies

I have found these fairies so enjoyable to make and I hope you will, too!

No two seem to turn out exactly alike – it is as if they take on characters of their own. This is a design that can be adapted in a number of ways to suit your requirements. Experiment with different hairstyles for instance, or make alternative hats, dresses and shoes. This design includes a wide range of techniques such as looping, spiralling and paper sticks, in addition to conventional quilling.

You will see from the variations that you can use the basic fairy as a starting point and have fun quilling tiny accessories for your fairies to hold.

You will need

Head, 2mm strips
Two pale pink strips, 450mm (18in) long

Small square of soft tissue paper

Body, 3mm strips
One dark pink strip, 300mm (11¾in) long

Hair, 1mm strips
Two golden brown strips, 450mm (18in) long

Dress, 3mm strips
Ten strips in 5 shades of pink (2 strips of each colour), 450mm (18in) long

One dark pink strip, 30mm (1¼in) long, for fringing

Arms
Two pieces of pale pink tissue paper, 25mm (1in) square

Hands, 2mm strips
Two pale pink strips, 56mm (2¼in) long

Legs
Four pieces of pale pink tissue paper, 32mm (1¼in) square

Feet, 3mm strips
Two dark pink strips, 112mm (4½in) long

Wings, 2mm strips
Three white strips, 450mm (18in) long

One dark pink strip, 450mm (18in) long

Tiara, 2mm strips
One dark pink strip, 300mm (11¾in) long

Other equipment
Extra fine-pointed felt-tip pens in black and pink

1 For the head, join two pale pink strips together end to end (see page 123), then roll the strip into a solid coil. Dome the coil and squeeze it into an oval shape.

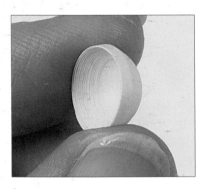

2 Make a tight ball out of soft tissue paper to fit snugly inside the head. Seal it with PVA glue, then glue it inside the fairy's head.

3 Make the body using a teardrop. Pinch out one side to create the waist.

4 Put a dab of glue on the rounded end of the body and push it on to the base of the head. Allow the glue to dry.

5 Now make the fairy's hair. Begin by creating two full-length spirals from the 1mm golden brown strips. Start on the top of her head in the centre, apply a strip of glue down the side of the head and attach a length of spiral.

6 Cut the spiral to the required length, then glue on the next section in the same way, gradually working your way around the head. Start each lock of hair from the same point on the top of the fairy's head.

7 Make sure the hair frames the face, without covering too much of it.

8 If your fairy is freestanding, make sure the back of the head is completely covered. (There is no need do this if she is to be mounted on a card or frame.)

9 If necessary, neaten the fairy's hair by trimming it.

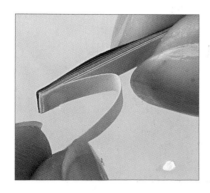

10 Begin the dress. Take the ten 3mm paper strips in five different shades of pink, two strips in each shade. Arrange them in order, from the lightest to the darkest shade. Glue the strips together, one on top of the other, at one end. Make a loop, approximately 10mm (½in) deep, in the first strip (this will form the inner part of the dress). Glue the loop in place at the top.

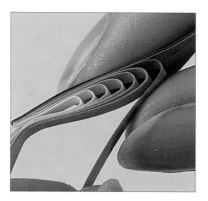

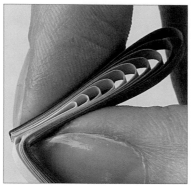

11 Form the remaining strips into loops in the same way, making them progressively longer.

12 When you have made all the loops, bend the strips back on themselves ready to start the next set of loops.

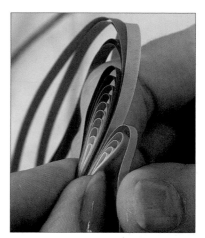

13 Start to form the second set of loops, matching the depth of the loops in the first set as closely as possible.

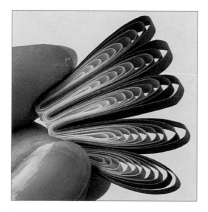

14 Make five sets of loops, and cut off the excess paper to finish.

15 Apply glue to the top of the skirt, ready to attach it to the fairy's body.

16 Push the skirt on to the end of the body and allow the glue to dry.

17 Take the 30mm (1¼in) length of 3mm paper strip and snip into it along one edge to create a fine fringe.

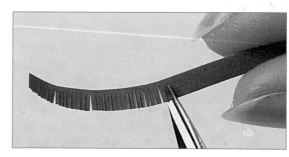

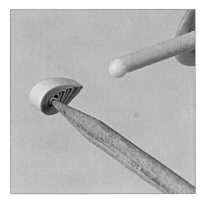

18 Use this to decorate the top of the fairy's dress. Apply dabs of glue around the top of the dress, lay the fringe over the top and secure it at the back.

19 Place a strip of glue along the inside edges of the two outer loops on either side of the fairy's dress, and push them together to hold the folds in place.

20 For the arms, make two paper sticks from 25mm (1in) square sheets of tissue paper. Make two teardrops for the hands, and glue one to the end of each arm.

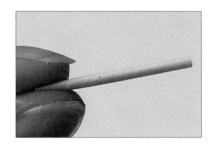

22 Make two more paper sticks for the legs using 32mm (1¼in) squares of tissue paper. Follow the same method as for the arms, though this time use two squares of tissue paper for each limb to make the legs thicker than the arms. Apply a dab of glue to one end of each leg and squash it flat. This makes it easier to attach the legs to the fairy's body.

21 Bend each arm in the middle to create an elbow.

23 Make two teardrops for the fairy's feet. Place a dab of glue at the tip of each one, and attach the unflattened end of each leg to a foot.

24 Place glue along the edges of the central loop, and insert the legs.

25 Put a dab of glue on the fairy's back and attach both arms. Leave the glue to dry.

26 To begin the wings, take a 2mm white paper strip and put a single loop in the end, approximately 10mm (½in) deep. Secure it with a dab of glue. Bend the paper strip back on itself, ready to form the next loop.

27 Create a total of nine loops for the upper wings, and six for the lower wings. There is no need to glue each loop. Make two upper wings using a full strip for each, and two lower wings using half a strip for each.

28 Push down on the tip of each wing to form it into the correct shape.

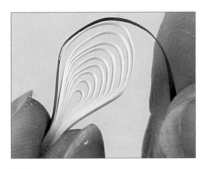

29 Apply glue around the outside of each wing, and attach a pink strip. Wrap it around once, then trim off the excess.

30 Glue each upper wing to a lower wing at their tips, then glue the two pairs of wings together. Allow the glue to dry.

31 Place a dab of glue in the centre of the wings and press the fairy down on them.

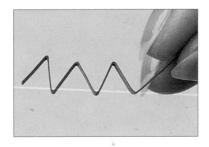

32 For the tiara, make a double-thickness 2mm strip, then when it is dry cut it down to 1mm. Form the strip into a concertina shape with six points. Cut off the excess.

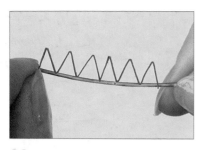

33 Apply a line of glue to a 40mm (1 ½in) length of the same double-thickness paper strip, even out the points in the concertina shape, and lay it on the strip. Allow the glue to dry thoroughly.

34 Bend the shape round into a circle to form a tiara. Glue the ends together, pushing down on them with the side of a cocktail stick to seal the join. Allow the glue to dry.

35 Put glue around the base of the tiara and attach it to the fairy's head.

36 Using extra fine-pointed felt-tip pens, draw on the fairy's face using two black dots for the eyes and a curved pink line for the mouth.

The completed fairy.

The basic fairy design can be easily adapted so that the fairies become angels — these would make a delightful addition to your Christmas tree! Only three loops are used for the dress instead of five, and the number of strips used has been increased to add length. Each wing is made in the same way as the basic fairy wing, but increased in size and pinched into a different shape.

Opposite

These green-fingered fairies hold a pot of lavender, a watering can and lavender in a paper trug. To make the trug, glue together 3mm-wide double-thickness strips in a curved shape, then edge the whole thing with another 3mm strip and add a double-thickness strip for the handle. The lavender is made from very thin double-thickness strips covered with glue at one end, and coated with mauve sprinkles, as for the chocolates (see page 128).

The flower pot is made from a tall dome, squashed flat at the base. Glue a loose coil inside then wedge the stems into it before adding some dark brown sprinkles for the soil (see page 128).

The watering can is made from silver-faced paper. Use a 10mm-wide strip for the main part of the can, glued round a large, 3mm-wide peg rolled from a 450mm (18in) long strip. Make a tapered tube for the spout section, finished off with a domed peg. Add handles made from 2mm-wide strips.

These cheerful baking fairies are armed with their own cooking utensils, including a tiny paper whisk! They also wear quilled aprons to protect their fairy clothes. They would make a charming gift for an enthusiastic chef.

The chefs' hats are made from a loose coil rolled from a 5mm-wide strip, 112mm (4½in) long. To make the top section, glue four 25mm (1in) strips in the centre to form a star. Roll each of the eight ends into the centre and remove the tool. Glue the coil into the open centre.

Large pegs have been used to make the jam, plate, saucepan and bowl – the bowl has been domed and then upturned. The 'mixture' inside the bowl is made from tiny curls, as for the chocolates (see page 128). Paper sticks have been used for handles, and the whisk is made from silver spirals formed into loops and gathered at the base. The 'bowl' of the wooden spoon is a small solid coil which has been domed slightly. The jam tarts are made in the same way, with added sprinkles, as for the chocolates (see page 128). The jam jar has been wrapped with clear sticky tape to make it look like glass. The aprons are formed from strips 1mm wide. They are made in two sections, then joined together at the waist with a narrow strip. A small semi-circle has been quilled for the pocket.

Quilled Borders & Motifs

by Judy Cardinal

I have always loved playing with colour and design, but sadly drawing and painting are not my forte. Quilling is therefore wonderful for me, as the range of colours and different types of paper available allow me to be really creative without the need to draw. I very rarely create the same design twice – a very different look can often be achieved by simply varying the size or the colours used. I hope, through this chapter, to encourage you to experiment and change your designs so that everything you create is your own unique piece of work.

It is not necessary to keep to the colours and forms found in nature – a floral motif in shades of white and blue can be very effective. Try red frogs for fun, or bright, clashing colours on an abstract bird or fish. Quilling can take your imagination anywhere you like, and nothing is wrong if it pleases you.

There are clear instructions at the beginning of the chapter on the materials and equipment you need to get started; the basic techniques involved; how to create a quilled motif; and how to arrange your borders and motifs on greetings cards, picture frames, gift boxes and so on. In the remainder of the chapter I have provided a variety of designs which I hope will excite and inspire you, giving you a source of ideas for your own quilling projects.

All the borders and motifs shown here, and on pages 164–183, are actual size, and have been made using 3mm wide paper strips; instructions for most are provided, apart from the simpler ones which I feel are self-explanatory. Templates for the more intricate designs are provided on pages 184–191.

Materials

Quilling is a creative but inexpensive craft requiring a basic starter kit of only quilling papers, a quilling tool, glue and card. As you progress, there are many beautiful papers to collect to add variety to your work, plus some extra pieces of equipment which can be useful.

Quilling papers

Quilling papers come in many colours, from delicate pastels to vibrant darker shades. Packs of papers are available in rainbow mixes, shades of the same colour or single colours. It is helpful as a beginner to start with a rainbow-mix pack of papers and progress to the shaded and single colours when you have developed your own style of quilling and know which colours you enjoy working with.

Papers come in a variety of widths, from 1mm up to 10mm wide. The usual width used is 3mm and this will be used throughout this chapter.

Instructions in this chapter are given as fractions of a basic 450mm (18in) strip (please refer to the conversion table on page 4).

Graduated papers

Graduated papers are very pale at each end of the strip and get progressively darker towards the centre. When coiled, they give a shaded effect to the quilled shapes, as illustrated on the daisy leaves below.

Metallic- and pearl-edged papers

Papers are available with a gold, silver or other metallic finish to the edge of the strip, and also with delicate, pearlescent edges. These papers come in a variety of colours and are particularly effective for Christmas quilling designs or for special celebrations such as weddings and anniversaries.

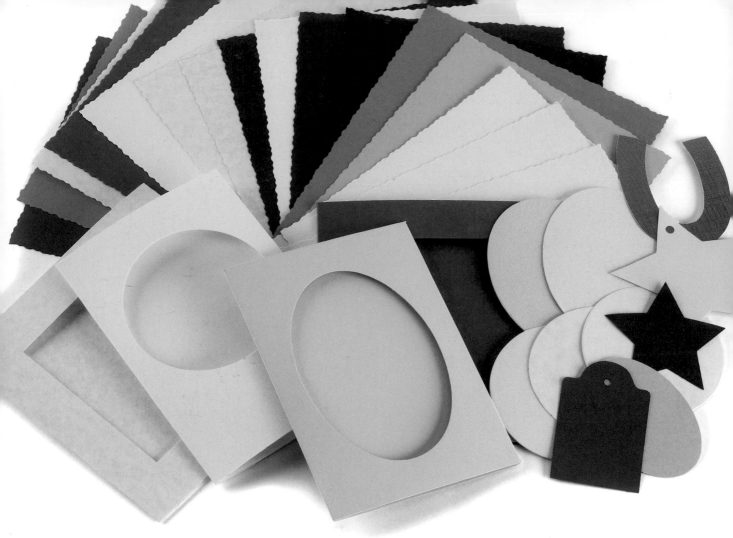

Card blanks, papers and card

Many colours and sizes of ready-scored blank cards can be bought from craft shops, or alternatively you can fold and score your own cards from sheets of cardstock. Quilling is enhanced if it is mounted on backing papers or on a card shape whose colour tones with that of the base card. It is helpful to have a good variety of colours to try the quilled shapes on before gluing down. It is not always the first combination of colours you try that is the most effective – be prepared to experiment.

Picture frames and gift boxes

Gift boxes come in many shapes and sizes and can make a gift really special if they are personalised by adding a quilled motif to the lid or the sides of the box. Many of the quilled borders in this chapter can be used around picture frames or mounts. These can be very effective if the quilling reflects the colours and subject of the photograph.

Quilling tools and equipment

There are several varieties of quilling tool on the market. I find the easiest to use are the wooden-handled tools with a fine-slot needle. These give a tight centre to the quilled shapes and are comfortable to use. Plastic and metal tools are also available.

Good quality PVA glue is the best adhesive to use as it dries clear. It can be applied with a cocktail stick or a fine-tip glue applicator.

A quilling board of cork or fibreboard (or any board into which you can stick pins) should be used to assemble your design. Take care to avoid gluing your work to the board, and place a piece of white paper on the board first to keep it clean. If you are using a template, protect it with a sheet of greaseproof or tracing paper.

A selection of short and long round-headed pins and dressmaking pins is useful for holding the different parts of your motif in place as you assemble it. You will also need a small, sharp pair of scissors, a round-ended knife to loosen any quilled shapes that may get stuck to the board, a pair of tweezers for manipulating small

Embellishments

Optional embellishments for quilled designs are ribbons, pearl or seed beads, joggle eyes and stickers. The easiest way to attach beads to your work is to place a dot of glue where it is needed using a cocktail stick, and then drop the bead on to the glue.

Basic techniques

The craft of quilling essentially involves coiling narrow strips of paper to form intricate shapes and patterns. Most shapes are formed from a basic closed coil. There are also more advanced quilling techniques, such as filigree quilling where the shapes are not glued closed, quilled roses and wheatears (single looping). These are all described on the following eight pages.

Basic closed coil

The size of the basic closed coil is varied by using different lengths of quilling paper. When coiling, wind the tool either towards you or away from you, whichever comes naturally.

Tip

While coiling, cover the end of the tool with the index finger of your other hand to stop the paper coil slipping off, and hold the paper firmly between your thumb and third finger to maintain tension.

1 Insert the end of the paper strip into the slot at the end of the quilling tool.

2 Start to turn the quilling tool so that the paper winds tightly around it.

3 When you come to the end of the strip, loosen the coil slightly and remove the quilling tool, allowing the coil to unwind like a spring.

4 Put a small dab of PVA glue on the end of the paper to seal the coil. Make sure you spread the glue right to the edge of the paper.

5 Seal the coil by pressing down lightly on the join with your finger.

Shapes

Starting with the basic closed coil, various shapes can be formed by simply pinching and shaping it with the fingers.

A basic closed coil.

Teardrop

Pinch the basic closed coil at one end using your thumb and forefinger.

Leaf

Pinch the basic closed coil at both ends and twist.

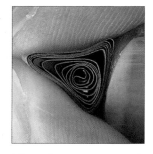

Triangle

Form the coil into a triangle using three fingers, then pinch out one corner and flatten the other side.

Bell

Hold the basic closed coil with both hands, slide your forefingers down to form the sides, then pinch out the two corners at the base of the bell.

Square

Squeeze the basic closed coil between the thumb and forefinger of each hand to form an even-sided diamond.

Holly leaf

Pinch both sides of the closed coil and then push the fingers together to form two more points.

Marquise

Pinch out the basic closed coil at both ends to form a long, thin shape.

Half moon

Pinch out each end, as you did for the marquise, then curl the shape into a crescent moon.

The basic shapes used in this chapter, all derived from the basic closed coil.

Peg

The peg is the only shape to be glued tightly while it is still on the quilling tool. A peg is often used to form flower centres or for candles on Christmas cards.

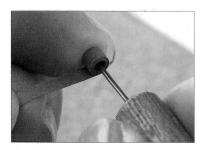

1 Form a basic closed coil, as shown on page 10.

2 Glue down the end of the paper while it is still wound tightly on the quilling tool.

3 Carefully remove the quilling tool, twisting it slightly as you do so to help loosen it.

4 Lay the peg on a flat surface, and flatten it with the end of the quilling tool.

The completed peg.

Each 'eye' on this beautiful peacock is a peg made from a ⅛ black strip, a ⅛ deep blue strip, a ¼ gold-edged white strip and a ¼ jade green strip joined together in series, then coiled starting with the black. The seven tail feathers are wheatears (see page 156), and the body is a tightly coiled teardrop made from two blue and two turquoise strips joined in parallel. The head is also a teardrop, made from a blue ½ strip and a turquoise ½ strip joined in parallel with a hole left in the centre for the eye, which is a loose peg shape squeezed into an oval made from a white ⅛ strip and a black ⅛ strip joined in series. The two feet are ¼ strip indented triangles and the head feathers are three ⅛ strips coiled down part of their length. (See template on page 188.)

Joining two strips

Two or more strips joined in series (end to end) can be used to make a peg of two or more colours, as seen in the feathers of the peacock on page 152. This is also a very effective way to introduce colour variation within a flower petal or leaf. Two strips joined in parallel (one on top of the other) gives a multicoloured effect to a coil. Use two shades of the same colour for a more subtle effect, or two contrasting colours for impact.

Joining two strips in parallel

 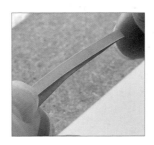

1 Apply glue to the end of one strip.

2 Glue the two strips together, one on top of the other.

Joining two strips in series

1 Apply glue to the end of one strip.

2 Lay the glued end on top of the end of the other strip.

Eccentric coiling

In eccentric coils, the centre of the coil is pulled out to one side of the shape. They are often used for the bodies of animals or party balloons.

1 Form a basic closed coil. Insert a tall pin in the quilling board and place the coil next to it. Insert a second pin in the centre of the coil.

2 Pull the second pin towards the first, drawing the centre of the coil to one side.

3 Apply glue at the base of the eccentric coil (where the coils are closest together).

4 When the glue is dry, remove the pins.

Filigree quilling

Filigree quilling is a more delicate style of quilling in which the coils are not glued into a basic closed coil. Shapes are formed by first folding a paper strip in half and then coiling the end of the strip with a quilling tool and releasing it. I find it best to coil down to the fold or crease in the paper strip before removing the tool, and then teasing out the coil to the required length. When attaching filigree coils to a background, make sure the glue is applied to every part of the shape.

Heart

Hearts are usually made using a ¼ strip.

1 Fold the paper strip in half and crease it at the bottom.

2 Coil one side of the paper strip inwards, towards the centre of the V, using a quilling tool.

3 Remove the quilling tool, and coil the other side of the paper strip inwards, to the same depth.

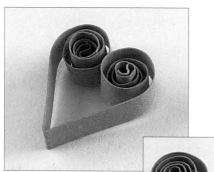

A completed heart.

A completed heart.

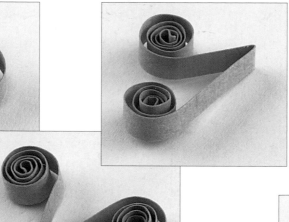

V coil

Made in the same way as a heart, but with the coils formed outwards.

Scroll

Both coils are formed in the same direction, one higher than the other.

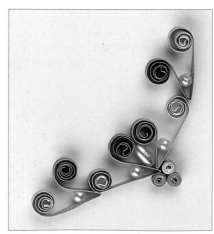

I have made this corner filigree from four ¼ strip scroll shapes and three ⅛ strip pegs in graduated purple and pink papers. Once glued down, I decorated the motif with 3mm pearl beads.

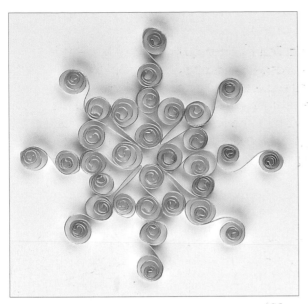

This delicate silver snowflake is made of ¼ strip S and V coils using silver-edged white paper. There is a template for this shape on page 190.

S coil

1 Find the central point of the paper strip by folding it in half, but do not crease it.

2 Coil both ends of the paper down to the centre to form an S shape.

P coil

A completed P coil.

Fold the paper strip in half, crease it, and coil both ends together using a quilling tool, working towards the fold. The strip forming the inner coil will bend away from the other as you work.

This flamboyant bird has a teardrop-shape body made from two strips joined together in parallel, a ¼ strip teardrop head and a ½ strip leaf-shape neck. The rest of the motif is made from various filigree shapes, and decorated with pearl beads.

Wheatears (single looping)

These are very useful shapes, formed without the quilling tool, which can be made any size and shaped with the fingers. Always start with a full-length strip of paper and trim off any excess when you have made the required number of loops.

1 Make a loop at one end of the paper strip.

2 Apply glue along the edge of the paper.

3 Glue the ends of the loop together, then start to wrap the paper around the loop to form the second loop.

4 Apply glue to the base of the second loop.

5 Continue making loops in the paper, applying glue at the base of each loop before moving on to the next. When you have made the desired number of loops, cut off the paper strip just below the base, fold over the excess paper and glue it in position.

The completed loops.

This shape is formed by pinching the base and gently squeezing the loops as you slide your fingers up the shape and pinch the top, forming an elongated leaf shape.

For a wing or petal shape, form a leaf shape, then push the tips back towards each other.

Twist the ends of the leaf shape for a more interesting effect.

Quilled roses

Quilled roses can be made with any width of paper, but for more delicate ones use 3mm wide strips. Roses look especially realistic when made with graduated papers, but there is plenty of scope to use your imagination and experiment with different colours. Use green paper strips to make cabbages and lettuces!

1 Form the centre of the rose by turning the paper strip once around the quilling tool and gluing it in place.

2 Fold the paper down towards the handle of the quilling tool, forming an accurate right angle.

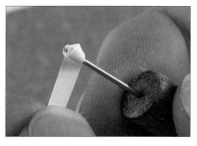

3 Roll the paper strip loosely over the fold so that you do not crush the rose shape as it forms. Continue rolling until the paper is at right angles to the quilling tool.

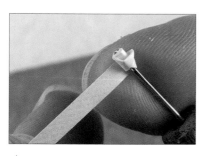

4 Continue folding and coiling, holding the petals in place with your forefinger as you work.

5 As you fold and coil, make sure the rose shape is tight at the base and fans out towards the top.

6 When your rose is the desired size, remove the quilling tool. The coils will unwind slightly, and the rose will open out.

7 Trim off the excess paper using a diagonal cut, add a dab of glue to the end of the paper and secure it on the back of the rose.

A completed rose.

Making borders and motifs

When making a motif, first quill all the shapes required. More complicated designs will need a template, which can be protected from glue by covering it with either greaseproof or tracing paper. Secure your shapes on a quilling board using pins to stop them moving around, and glue them together. Apply glue to the sides of the shapes so that the completed motif does not become stuck to the board and can be lifted off easily. Compare your motif on various backgrounds before deciding on which one to use, and then glue it in place.

Borders are usually composed of different elements. Make each element separately, then arrange them on your background before gluing them down. Always start at the centre of the border and work outwards to ensure the shapes are evenly spaced.

You will need

For the candle motif:

- Five x ½ strip red pegs
- One x ⅛ strip yellow teardrop
- One x ¼ strip cream scroll
- Three x ¼ strip gold-edged green holly-leaf shapes
- Three x ⅛ strip red pegs
- Quilling board
- Scrap sheet of white paper
- Four drawing pins
- Selection of long and short round-headed pins
- Copy of the template

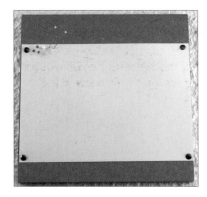

1 Begin by preparing your work surface. Pin a sheet of paper on to your quilling board. Keep some pins handy for holding your quilled shapes in place as you work.

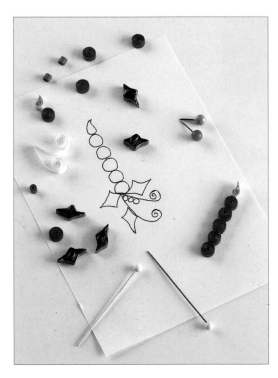

2 Gather together everything you need to make the motif or border, including the quilled shapes, template and pins.

Template for the motif (reproduced actual size).

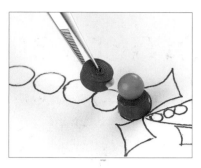

3 Pin the template to the board, and pin on the peg at the base of the candle using a round-headed pin. Position the peg so that the join will be hidden by the second peg.

4 Put a dab of glue on a second peg so that it covers the join, and attach it to the first.

5 Complete the candle following this method, finishing with the flame at the top. Use as many pins as you need.

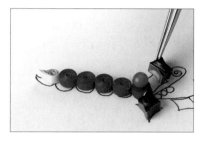

6 Arrange two leaves and the filigree at the base of the candle. Make sure you are happy with the arrangement before gluing them down.

7 Glue the two leaves in place, applying the glue to the sides of the leaves where they touch the candle.

8 Put a dab of glue along the folded edge of the filigree shape and attach it to the leaves. Attach the remaining elements in the same way.

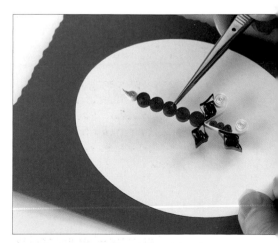

9 When dry, remove the pin and lift the completed motif off the template, loosening it first with the tip of a round-ended knife if necessary.

10 Apply glue to the back of the motif, making sure you cover every element. You can also do this by dipping a cocktail stick in glue and rolling it back and forth across the back of the motif.

11 Attach the motif to your chosen background.

Imagine a themed Christmas table with the place cards and napkin rings decorated with quilled motifs, or coordinating gift tags, gift boxes, Christmas cards and tree decorations. The photograph opposite shows just some of the ways you can use quilled designs to create a themed 'look' for Christmas. Extend this idea to other celebrations to make them extra special, such as birthdays, anniversaries and weddings.

Using borders and motifs

You can use borders and motifs as accents to enhance larger quilled projects, or they can be mounted to form the main subject of a greetings card, gift tag, place card or picture frame. On these two pages are some ideas for laying out borders and motifs. Most of them can be adapted to suit any size or style of background, so simply use your imagination and have fun!

Roses create a perfect border around an aperture card, either going part of the way round (as shown above), or encircling it completely.

Many of the motifs in this chapter can be extended to form a long border down the side of a card, for example by adding the line of leaves above and below this owl motif.

Small motifs at opposite corners of a card create a delicate look for a wedding invitation, greetings card or place card.

Placing small motifs at opposite corners that echo the main design in the centre of a card can be very effective.

Filigree borders can be used along two sides of a card or frame, or extended to go all the way round the edge.

A motif or border placed in a corner and extending part of the way round two sides of a card looks very effective, especially when echoed by a smaller version in the opposite corner.

Four tiny, themed motifs placed in the corners of a card can be used to border an invitation or thank-you card, or a larger quilled motif in the centre of a greetings card.

These quilled motifs follow the curve of an oval aperture. This design could be repeated in the opposite corner.

Individual quilled motifs can be placed in a line along the bottom edge of a landscape card to form an interesting and lively border.

Flowers

Quilling flowers is a joy, as such a huge range of colours and forms can be used and combined. Recreate real flowers from nature, or design complete fantasy flowers in which any combination of colours can be used.

Daisy motif

The daisy centre is a ¼ strip yellow peg and the seven petals are ⅓ strip white marquises. The leaves are six ½ strip green marquises and a ¼ strip green scroll. This design is decorated with 3mm pearl beads. (See template on page 188.)

Blue fantasy flower

This flower is made with three ⅛ strip pegs (two turquoise and one deep blue), two ½ strip deep blue leaf shapes, two ¼ strip pale blue leaf shapes, a ¼ strip turquoise teardrop and a ¼ strip turquoise scroll. It is finished with four 3mm pearl beads. (See template on page 188.)

Yellow fantasy flower

Two ½ strip orange leaf shapes, two ¼ strip pale yellow leaf shapes, a ¼ strip central dark yellow teardrop and a ¼ strip pale green scroll have been used to make this flower. It is decorated with 3mm pearl beads and elongated pearl beads. (See template on page 188.)

Pink and green fantasy flower

The pink and green fantasy flower has two ½ strip pale green leaf shapes, a ¼ strip pink teardrop in the centre and two ¼ strip 'V' shape filigree scrolls. Pearl beads are used for decoration. (See template on page 188.)

Lilac fantasy flower

The lilac fantasy flower has four ½ strip leaf shapes in shades of lilac, and a ¼ strip pale green scroll. It is decorated with round and elongated pearl beads. (See template on page 188.)

Daisy border

The small blue flowers are made of five ⅛ strip blue pegs around a ⅛ strip yellow peg centre. The daisies have ¼ strip yellow peg centres, with seven ⅛ strip white marquises for petals. The connecting pale yellow leaf shapes are ⅛ and ¼ strips.

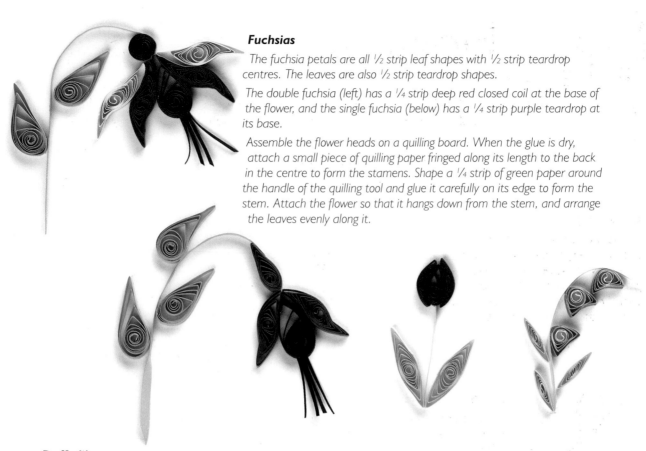

Fuchsias

The fuchsia petals are all ½ strip leaf shapes with ½ strip teardrop centres. The leaves are also ½ strip teardrop shapes.

The double fuchsia (left) has a ¼ strip deep red closed coil at the base of the flower, and the single fuchsia (below) has a ¼ strip purple teardrop at its base.

Assemble the flower heads on a quilling board. When the glue is dry, attach a small piece of quilling paper fringed along its length to the back in the centre to form the stamens. Shape a ¼ strip of green paper around the handle of the quilling tool and glue it carefully on its edge to form the stem. Attach the flower so that it hangs down from the stem, and arrange the leaves evenly along it.

Daffodils

Daffodil leaves can be made from either wheatears (the number of loops varied to make different lengths of leaf) or full-strip leaf shapes. Each stem is made from a ¼ strip of green paper, coiled at one end for a quarter of its length and glued into a teardrop shape. The rest of the strip becomes the stem, which can be trimmed to the required length.

The petals of the left-hand flower are four ¼ strip yellow leaf shapes with a ¼ strip deep yellow holly-leaf shape centre. The central daffodil has ¼ strip leaf-shape petals and an orange ¼ strip holly-leaf shape centre. Each flower head of the daffodil clump on the right is made of two ¼ strip yellow teardrops with a ¼ strip pale yellow half-moon centre.

Roses

Roses make beautiful designs, especially for romantic celebrations such as anniversaries, weddings and Valentine's Day. They look particularly effective when made using graduated papers.

Designs that include roses should first be laid out on a quilling board to ensure the elements are positioned correctly, then glued together on your chosen background. Start with the main roses and gradually work outwards, incorporating any leaves, scrolls or other elements. Have fun combining different-coloured roses and leaves, and decorate your creations with beads and pegs. Leaves can be marquise- or leaf-shaped and made using ¼ or ⅛ strips.

White rose motif

Glue three roses to the card, a ¼ strip 'V' coil which has one end longer than the other, four ½ strip leaves and 3mm pearl bead decorations.

Rose bouquet

Draw a faint circle, the size of an eggcup, on to the card. Fill this shape with roses, covering the pencil marks. Arrange a ¼ strip green scroll and two ⅛ strips folded in half to make ribbons hanging down from the base of the bouquet. Place nine ⅛ strip green teardrop-shape leaves evenly around the outside of the bouquet.

Rose trellis

Glue a trellis of beige papers flat on the card using two uprights placed 1cm (½in) apart, one 13cm (5in) long and the other 10cm (4in) long. Attach two cross bars, 3cm (1½in) long, diagonally across at the top and the bottom.

Make a selection of nine roses, sixteen ⅛ strip teardrop leaves and tendrils made from ⅛ strips coiled along half their length. Assemble the design from the base upwards.

Red rose corner spray

This border can be used around any shaped aperture or the corner of a card. Try starting with a deep colour and make the roses progressively paler. Build up the design starting at one end, placing two ¼ strip marquise leaves between each rose.

Pink rose corner spray

This design uses graduated paper strips, giving a delicately shaded effect. You will need six roses – three large and three smaller buds, eleven ¼ strip leaves and two ¼ strip scrolls. Starting with the three large roses, assemble the design outwards in both directions. This design can be placed around a single corner of a card, or on diagonally opposite corners.

Rose garland

Draw lightly around a small cup with an embossing tool to mark the card. Make nine roses in different shades of pink and four deep red roses. Quill nine ¼ strip 'S' coils, seven ¼ strip leaves and two ¼ strip scrolls using green paper. Arrange the scrolls and roses evenly around the circle, starting at its base, leaving a gap just off-centre at the top and bottom of the design. Place scrolls, roses and leaves in these gaps to form motifs at the top and bottom of the garland. Adjust the number of roses and leaves if necessary.

Pink rose corner motif

This motif is quilled using graduated papers and decorated with 3mm pearl beads. The leaves and scroll are all made with ¼ strips.

The Pond

Imagine a country pond on a summer's day, teeming with life – dragonflies hovering above it, ducks swimming and diving for food, colourful irises growing on its banks, frogs hiding under rocks and in the undergrowth, not to mention the fish swimming in the water itself. The picture I've just painted gave me inspiration for the motifs and borders on this page, which could be combined to create a whole pond-life scene.

Goldfish

The bodies of the fish are one yellow strip and one orange strip joined at the ends, one on top of the other, and rolled together in parallel to form a teardrop. The fins are ¼ strip triangles. and both the tail variations use ¼ strips. The tail of the left-hand fish is four ¼ strip leaf shapes in yellows and oranges, and that of the right-hand fish is two ¼ strip 'V' coils nestled one inside the other. Add joggle eyes or quill a ⅛ strip peg for an eye.

You can achieve some wonderful effects by using different shades of paper quilled in parallel for the bodies, or perhaps use more exotic colours and designs to quill a selection of tropical fish!

Frog border

Frogs are great fun – you can change their characters by the twist of the mouth or the set of their eyes! The larger frog on the left has a body of one full-strip green eccentric coil, two upper legs of ½ strip teardrops and two lower legs of ¼ strip teardrops. The mouth is a yellow ½ strip joined in series with a green ½ strip, coiled into a leaf shape starting with the yellow. Each eye is a black ¼ strip joined in series with a yellow ¼ strip and a green ¼ strip, coiled into a peg starting with the black. The smaller frogs are made in the same way, but with no upper legs and all the dimensions halved. Give them either a leaf-shape mouth or a marquise-shape mouth. To assemble the frogs, start by pinning down the mouth and build the rest of the design around it.

The bulrushes are wheatear leaves of varying lengths with stems cut to length and glued on their edges. The flower heads are ¼ strip leaf shapes, as is the water. To finish, add butterfly stickers, or quill your own butterflies following the instructions on pages 170–171.

Templates are provided for the frogs on page 189.

Duck border

These playful ducks are all quilled in the same way, but the shapes are positioned differently on the ½ and ¼ strip leaf shapes which form the water. The ducks' bodies are ½ strip teardrops and their heads are ¼ strip closed coils. Pull the heads into a size that is in proportion to the bodies. Complete the ducks with ¼ strip teardrop wings, ⅛ strip triangular feet, and a ¹⁄₁₆ strip teardrop beak. Assemble the ducks on a quilling board, gluing the wings on top of the body if possible to give a three-dimensional effect.

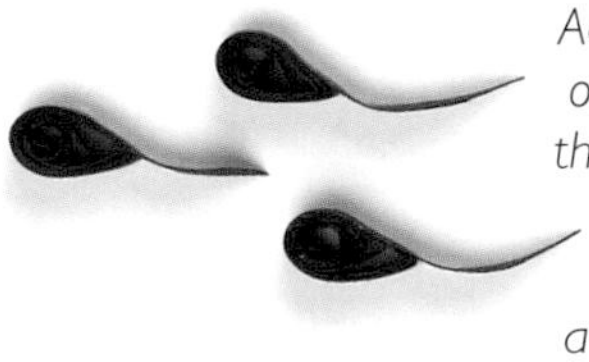

Tadpoles

Add these fun accents to the inside of a card or swimming along a gift tag with a pond-life theme! They are very simple to quill – just ¼ strips coiled almost to the end and then glued and shaped into a teardrop leaving a small tag for the tail.

Golden iris

The leaves are marquises (four ¾ strip and one ½ strip) quilled using graduated papers. The flower head, starting at the top, consists of two mid-yellow ½ strip teardrops, two light yellow ¼ strip leaf shapes, two mid-yellow ½ strip half moons and a central dark yellow ½ strip teardrop. (See template on page 189.)

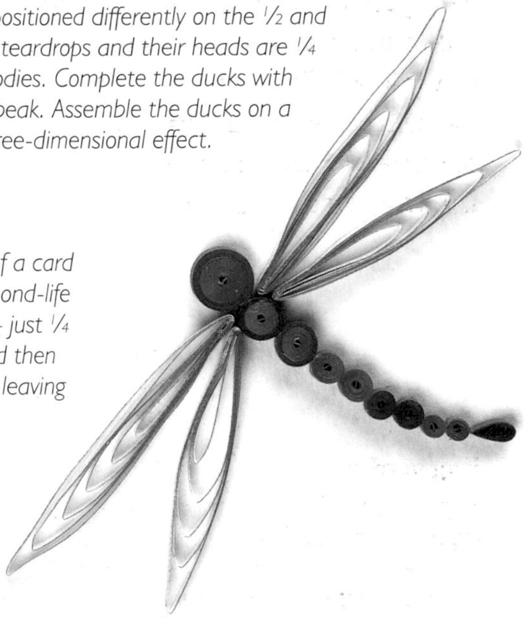

Dragonfly motif

I have used vibrant blues and turquoises for the dragonfly's body and silver-edged white paper for its wings. Assemble the head and body first, starting with the head. The head is a turquoise ½ strip joined in series with a deep blue ½ strip, coiled into a peg starting with the turquoise. Next are two pegs made in the same way with ¼ strips. The two pegs after that are ¼ strip turquoise, and the next two are ¼ strip dark blue. Lastly are two ⅛ turquoise strips and a ⅛ deep blue teardrop.

Both pairs of wings are wheatears, made long and pointed, with six loops for the top wings and five loops for the bottom wings.

Kissing ducks

These ducks make cute anniversary or Valentine's Day cards, or fun place cards for a wedding. Either make the ducks to the same dimensions as those in the border at the top of the page, or use ¼ strips for the bodies, ⅛ strips for the heads and ¹⁄₁₆ strips for the beaks. Add silver heart stickers to complete the design.

Butterflies

I enjoy quilling butterflies as I can really use my imagination and invent exciting colour combinations, wing and body shapes! All the different parts of the butterflies on these pages are interchangeable, and I hope you will experiment and create your own varieties of butterfly.

To make a wheatear wing, start with a complete paper strip and trim it once the wing is the required size. Leave it rounded, or shape it following the directions on page 156. The antennae are formed using either a scroll or a 'V' coil, or alternatively leave a 1 or 2cm (½ or ¾in) tag uncoiled when forming the head, glue the head shape together, then cut the excess paper in half lengthways and coil each half into a scroll or a 'V' shape.

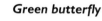

Jade and turquoise butterfly
The body is one turquoise strip and one jade strip joined in parallel and coiled into a leaf shape. The wing decorations are ¼ strip pegs and ¼ strip teardrops.

Three-wing butterfly
The body is a full-strip leaf shape, and the wing decorations are ½ strip teardrops and pearl beads.

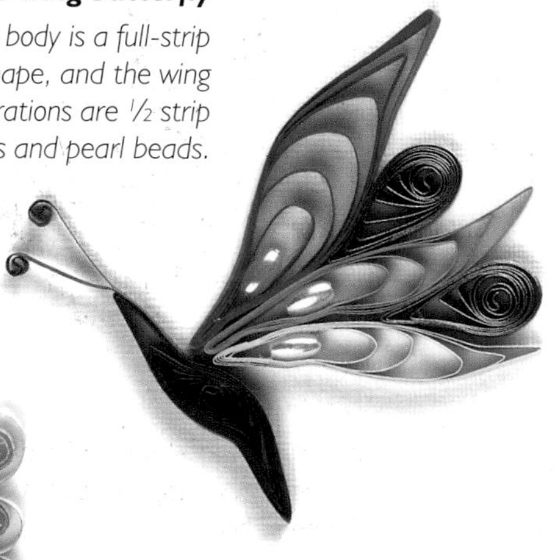

Green butterfly
The body is a full-strip teardrop, and the head is a ¼ strip closed coil. The wing decorations are ⅛ strip pegs and ¼ strip teardrops.

Peach butterfly
This delicate butterfly has three-looped wheatear top wings and ¼ strip teardrop bottom wings. The head is a ⅛ strip peg and the body is a ½ strip marquise, both of which are made from gold-edged paper. The flower spray has a ⅛ strip peg in the centre, and ⅛ strip teardrop petals and buds. The leaves are ¼ strip marquises. (See template on page 189.)

Pink and purple graduated butterfly

This butterfly is made using graduated papers. The top wings are ½ strip leaf shapes and the bottom wings are ⅓ strip teardrops. The body is a ½ strip marquise and the head is a ¼ strip peg.

Pointed-winged butterfly

The head is a ½ strip peg and the body consists of two ½ strip pegs, three ¼ strip pegs and two ⅛ strip pegs. Coloured seed beads have been used to decorate the wings.

Blue and silver butterfly

The body of this butterfly is a ½ strip teardrop made from silver-edged white paper, which is also used for the 'P' coil antennae. The top wings are ½ strip silver-edged white paper joined in series with ½ strip blue paper coiled into a teardrop shape, starting with the white. The bottom wings are ½ strip teardrops.

Pink butterfly

The body is a full-strip leaf shape. The wheatear wings are decorated with pearl beads.

Butterfly border

All these butterflies are made from graduated papers and have ⅓ strip top wings and ¼ strip bottom wings. The bodies are ⅓ strip marquises, and the wing shapes are either marquises or teardrops. The linking flowers are ⅛ pegs with ¼ strip marquise leaves.

Yellow butterfly

The head is a ¼ strip teardrop and the body is a ½ strip teardrop. Pearl beads are used to decorate the wings.

Christmas

Christmas motifs can be used in so many different ways, from cards and gift tags to tree and cake decorations. Try different colour schemes from the traditional green and red, such as blue and silver or white and gold.

Jingle bells border

First make three bells, each from one strip of paper. You also need six ¼ strip holly-leaf shapes and six ¼ strip scrolls made from gold-edged green papers. Decorate with gold and red 3mm beads after the design has been attached to the card. (See template on page 190.)

Blue and gold candle

This unusual colour combination also works well in more traditional red and green. The candle needs five ½ strip gold-edged blue pegs, though the length of the candle can be extended by using more pegs. The flame is a ¼ strip gold-edged white teardrop, the six holly leaves are each made from a ¼ gold-edged white strip, and there are two gold-edged blue scrolls and 3mm pearl beads to decorate.

Keep the candle straight on the quilling board by ruling on a pencil line as a guide. (See template on page 189.)

White Christmas tree

This tree is made with ten ½ strip teardrops using white, gold-edged paper. Three ⅛ strip teardrops and six ⅛ strip pegs are used for the decorations. The pot is one full-strip square shape and the star a ¼ strip holly shape.

Assemble this design from the base of the tree upwards, keeping the shape as symmetrical as possible. Glue on the decorations while the tree is still on the quilling board.

A smaller tree can be quilled using only three teardrops and a ¼ strip pot.

Christmas garland

This garland is made from ¼ strip holly shapes in two shades of green, gold-edged green and gold-edged cream, approximately five shapes in each colour, depending on the size of the garland. Draw a faint circle on your card and glue the holly shapes at varying angles around it, making sure you cover the pencil mark. Decorate the garland with a bow made from a long strip of red paper, and decorate it with red and gold seed beads.

Poinsettia

This poinsettia consists of two layers of quilling, each made on a quilling board and layered one on top of the other when dry. For the first layer, glue five red $\frac{1}{3}$ strip leaf-shape petals together evenly in a circle, then attach six gold-edged green $\frac{1}{3}$ strip leaf shapes between them. Layer two is a circle of five red $\frac{1}{4}$ strip leaf shapes. Complete the motif by adding gold seed beads on the top to form the central buds. (See template on page 189.)

Robin

This cheeky little robin can be repeated along the edge of a card to form a border or used as a single motif. The body is a $\frac{1}{2}$ strip teardrop, the tail a $\frac{1}{4}$ strip indented triangle and the head a $\frac{1}{4}$ strip closed coil. The robin's red breast is a $\frac{1}{2}$ strip half-moon shape, pinned closely to the body on a quilling board until the glue is dry. The legs are $\frac{1}{8}$ strip marquises and the tiny beak is a $\frac{1}{16}$ strip marquise. Decorate with two $\frac{1}{4}$ strip holly leaves, a $\frac{1}{4}$ strip scroll and red seed bead berries. (See template on page 190.)

Angels border

The stars, wings and halos are all quilled with gold-edged cream paper strips, the bodies and heads are white and the feet palest pink. $\frac{1}{4}$ strip holly-leaf shapes are used for the linking stars, and each angel has a $\frac{1}{2}$ strip triangular body with a $\frac{1}{4}$ strip closed coil head pulled into a size that is in proportion to the body. The wings are $\frac{1}{4}$ strip teardrops, the haloes $\frac{1}{8}$ strip marquises and the feet $\frac{1}{8}$ strip pegs.

Gold candles and holly border

This border can be extended with extra scrolls and holly. First make the two candles on the quilling board, one with five and one with four pegs and each made of $\frac{1}{2}$ strip gold-edged paper. The flames are $\frac{1}{4}$ strip leaf shapes. Quill the rest of the shapes – four deep red roses, three cream roses, nine $\frac{1}{2}$ strip gold-edged green holly leaves, two scrolls and two 'V' coils in gold-edged cream paper – then arrange the design on the quilling board without gluing before attaching it to your chosen background.

Flying High!

These fun motifs and borders make colourful decorations for children's birthday cards and party invitations.

Kite motif

Children's kites can be many different colours and the tail can be extended to form a colourful border. For this kite you will need two ½ strip triangles (one red and one orange), two full-strip triangles in the same colours and two ¼ strip yellow triangles. The tail is made from six ¼ strip triangles attached in pairs either side of a 10cm (4in) long paper strip glued along its edge. (See template on page 190.)

Party balloon border

All the balloons in this border are ½ strip closed coils with a 1 or 2cm (½ or ¾in) tag left uncoiled for the string. The musical notes are ⅛ strip pegs with a short tag left uncoiled. Arrange the shapes at varying angles on the card, and finish by decorating with star stickers.

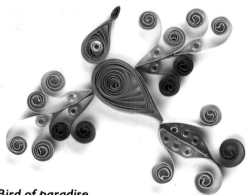

Bird of paradise

The bird's body is a full-strip teardrop shape, its head is a ¼ strip teardrop and the beak is a ¹⁄₁₆ strip teardrop. Both wings are formed from three ¼ strip scrolls, and the tail is a ¼ strip 'V' coil and two ¼ strip 'P' coils. I have used different blues throughout and 3mm beads for the eye and decorations. I have deliberately glued the beads with their holes uppermost for an unusual effect. (See template on page 190.)

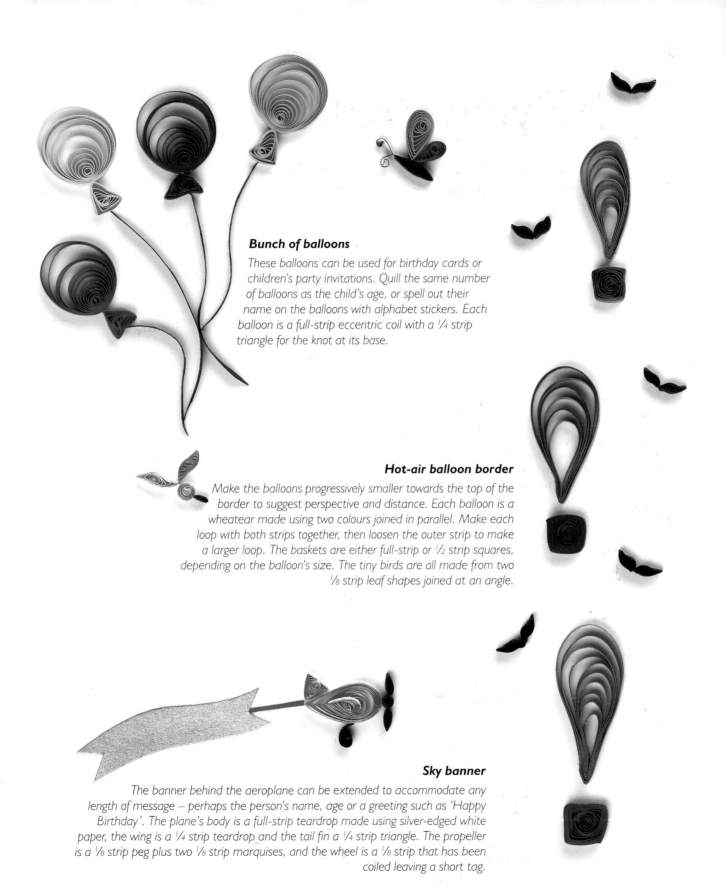

Bunch of balloons

These balloons can be used for birthday cards or children's party invitations. Quill the same number of balloons as the child's age, or spell out their name on the balloons with alphabet stickers. Each balloon is a full-strip eccentric coil with a $1/4$ strip triangle for the knot at its base.

Hot-air balloon border

Make the balloons progressively smaller towards the top of the border to suggest perspective and distance. Each balloon is a wheatear made using two colours joined in parallel. Make each loop with both strips together, then loosen the outer strip to make a larger loop. The baskets are either full-strip or $1/2$ strip squares, depending on the balloon's size. The tiny birds are all made from two $1/8$ strip leaf shapes joined at an angle.

Sky banner

The banner behind the aeroplane can be extended to accommodate any length of message – perhaps the person's name, age or a greeting such as 'Happy Birthday'. The plane's body is a full-strip teardrop made using silver-edged white paper, the wing is a $1/4$ strip teardrop and the tail fin a $1/4$ strip triangle. The propeller is a $1/8$ strip peg plus two $1/8$ strip marquises, and the wheel is a $1/8$ strip that has been coiled leaving a short tag.

The Sky

The theme of these two pages includes spaceships, fireworks, suns, moons and stars – all suitable for children's party invitations (particularly bonfire parties) and greetings cards. These designs work very well with metallic-edged papers, and can be made more dramatic by placing them on dark-coloured backgrounds.

Spaceship

This fun spaceship is made with silver-edged white paper and has black antennae and yellow windows. The body is made from a full-strip marquise and a 1/2 strip half moon. Each of the three legs is a 1/8 strip marquise and a 1/8 strip peg.

The three windows are 1/8 strip pegs glued on to the main body of the spaceship, and the antennae are 1/8 pegs with a small tag left uncoiled.

Rocket

The body of the rocket is quilled from metallic-edged red and green papers. The central part is a full-strip green rectangle, the nose cone is a 1/2 strip red triangle and the base is a 1/2 strip red square. Glue a paper strip 3cm (1 1/4in) long behind the rocket and arrange eight 1/8 strip marquises along it in red, yellow and orange.

Moons and stars border

This border looks particularly good on a deep blue background with white silver-edged stars. Try placing it around an oval aperture. I have used 1/4 strip gold-edged cream paper quilled into a holly-leaf shape for the stars, and then added extra small sticker stars. The moons are 1/2 strip half-moon shapes.

Silver snowflake

This delicate silver snowflake is made of 1/4 strip 'S' and 'V' coils using silver-edged white paper. (See template on page 190.)

Sun

Use different reds, oranges and yellows for this sun, or alternatively make it using a single colour. The sun itself is a full-strip eccentric coil. The rays are formed using six orange $\frac{1}{3}$ strip leaf shapes spaced evenly around the centre, and nine $\frac{1}{4}$ strip leaf shapes in shades of yellow placed randomly between them.

Filigree cloud

Clouds can be made any shape or size. I have used $\frac{1}{4}$ strip scrolls for this cloud, placed randomly on the background. Fill any awkward spaces using $\frac{1}{8}$ strip closed coils. The birds are $\frac{1}{4}$ strip leaf shapes and $\frac{1}{8}$ strip pegs.

Angel

This angel also works well quilled all in white, and the same design could be used to make a fairy. The angel's skirt is four wheatears, each with four loops, between which are $\frac{1}{4}$ strip teardrops. Her body is a $\frac{1}{2}$ strip teardrop, her face a full-strip closed coil (pulled to size), and her hair $\frac{1}{8}$ strip 'S' coils. Her wings each consist of a $\frac{1}{2}$ strip teardrop and a $\frac{1}{4}$ strip teardrop. (See template on page 191.)

Golden star

This star is made from gold-edged cream paper, and is also effective in pale yellow or gold-edged white paper. In the centre is a $\frac{1}{2}$ strip square shape and around this are eight triangles, four hearts and eight marquises, all $\frac{1}{4}$ strip. Keep this star symmetrical by constructing it on a sheet of graph paper, or use two rules placed at right angles to each other as a guide. (See template on page 191.)

The Plough

I have arranged these stars, each a $\frac{1}{8}$ strip holly leaf, in the shape of the constellation The Plough.

Weddings

A wedding day is very special, and what could be more wonderful than to quill coordinating invitations, orders of service, place cards and menus. Enhance the wedding photographs by quilling a border around the frame, or create a memory box for all the wedding mementoes. A quilled card sent to the bride and groom will be treasured for always.

Lucky horseshoe

I have decorated this horseshoe using roses in various shades of pink with ⅛ teardrop shapes for the leaves.

Match the colour of the roses to the bridesmaids' dresses or to the general theme of the wedding. (Use this picture as a template for the horseshoe shape.)

Champagne glasses

I made these using white silver-edged paper strips. The line of bubbles could be extended to form a border. For each glass use a full-strip triangle and two ¼ strip marquises. For the bubbles use ⅛ strip pegs and 3mm pearl beads.

Wedding rings

The two wedding rings would work well as a central motif, with the flowers extending either side. I have used one strip of gold-edged paper for the rings, coiled around a thick pen. The roses are made using graduated paper, and the leaves are each ⅛ strip teardrops. Assemble the design on your card or other background by first gluing the rings in the centre, followed by the roses, and then arranging the leaves in between.

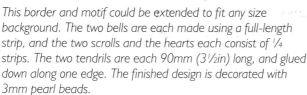

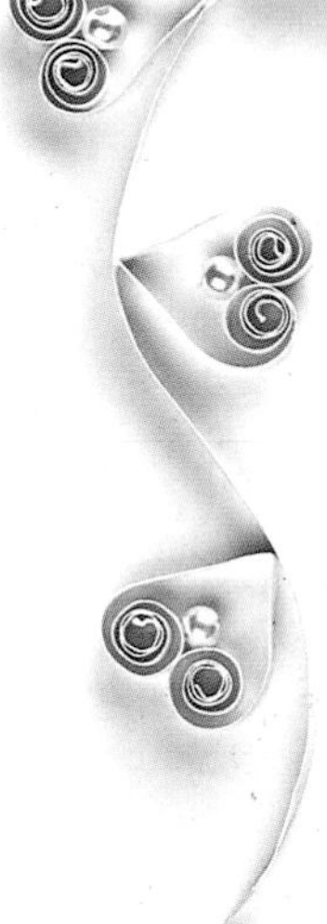

Bells and hearts

This border and motif could be extended to fit any size background. The two bells are each made using a full-length strip, and the two scrolls and the hearts each consist of ¼ strips. The two tendrils are each 90mm (3½in) long, and glued down along one edge. The finished design is decorated with 3mm pearl beads.

Bride

The bride's skirt is made from three wheatears, each with six loops, and two ¼ strip teardrops placed between them. Her body is a ½ strip teardrop. Her hat consists of a ½ strip leaf shape for the brim; a ¼ strip half moon for the crown (shaped to fit) and a ¼ strip scroll for the ribbon. The flowers in her bouquet are ¹⁄₁₆ strip pegs and the leaves ¹⁄₁₆ strip teardrops. (See template on page 191.)

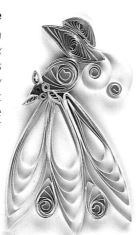

Ribbon and roses border

The bow at the top of this border is made from two ½ strip and two ¼ strip teardrops and a ¼ strip 'V' coil. Glue a length of quilling paper flat on the card and attach groups of roses at regular intervals along it. The ⅛ strip leaves and the ¼ strip scroll are added at the end to complete the design.

Dove

This delicate motif would work well on place cards. For the dove use a ½ strip teardrop for the body; a ½ strip triangle for the tail; a ½ strip closed coil for the head (pulled to size); a ⅛ strip teardrop for the beak; and a ½ strip teardrop for each wing. The two hearts are ¼ strip filigrees.

Babies

The arrival of a new baby is so special that everyone likes to send a card that the proud parents can cherish for always. These borders and motifs are suitable for birth and christening cards, birth announcements or perhaps scrapbook pages of the new baby. Personalise the card by adding the baby's name and birth date using stickers.

Cradle in the flowers

The flower spray is made from four $1/4$ strip scrolls and seven $1/4$ strip leaves, all in two shades of green. The flower buds consist of three $1/4$ strip and three $1/8$ strip teardrops in white. It is decorated with 3mm pearl beads. The cradle is a full-strip half moon in silver-edged white paper with a $1/2$ strip 'V' coil handle. (See template on page 191.)

Blue pram

The body of the pram consists of $1 1/2$ strips joined in series and quilled into a half moon, and the hood is a full-strip half moon. The wheels are $1/2$ strip closed coils supported on a $1/4$ strip 'S' coil, and the handle is a $1/4$ strip scroll. The hood is decorated with $1/8$ pegs alternating with 3mm blue beads.

Stork and baby

For the stork I have used a full-strip teardrop for the body, a $1/4$ strip teardrop for the head, and a $1/4$ strip triangle for the beak. Use a $1/4$ strip coiled halfway along its length and glued into a teardrop for the legs and feet. The eye is a $1/8$ strip peg. The baby consists of a $1/4$ strip closed coil head, and a $1/2$ strip teardrop and two $1/4$ strip teardrops shaped around each other for the shawl.

Baby's bonnet

This simple motif is a full-strip half moon with a ribbon glued on to one corner. The flower is made from $1/8$ strip pegs.

Teddy bear border

Each of the teddies has a $1/2$ strip closed coil body, a $1/4$ strip closed coil head, $1/8$ strip closed coil ears and $1/8$ strip teardrop arms and legs. The rattles have $1/4$ strip teardrop handles, and a peg consisting of a white $1/4$ strip and a pink $1/4$ strip joined in series. The flowers and connecting pegs are all made from $1/8$ strips. Any simple motifs could be incorporated into this border, perhaps using various shades of pink for a girl and blues for a boy.

Stork and crib

This stork flying in with the baby consists of two wings made from full-strip leaf shapes, a ½ strip teardrop head and a ¼ strip leaf-shape beak. The legs are made from a ½ strip folded in half, and each end coiled along half its length and glued into a teardrop. The baby basket is a ½ strip half-moon shape with a 'V' coil handle.

Pink crib

The body of the crib is 1 ½ strips joined in series and quilled into a half moon. The hood is a full-strip half moon decorated with two ⅛ strip 'S' coils, the legs are a ¼ strip 'V' coil and the blanket a ½ strip marquise.

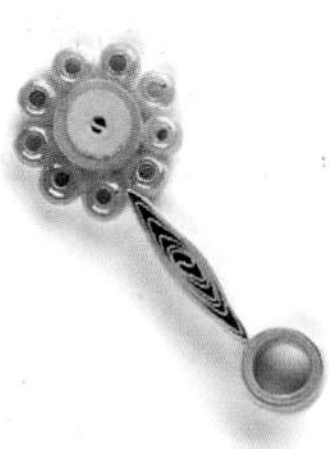

Baby border

Each of the elements in this border could also be used as individual motifs.

The safety pins are ¼ strips coiled halfway along their length, and then allowed to uncoil slightly and glued into a small closed coil. The rest of the strip is bent round to make a safety-pin shape and glued to the closed coil. A ⅛ strip peg is glued into the base of the pin.

The rattles are the same as those in the teddy bear border on the facing page, and the baby bottles are a full-strip rectangle, with a lid made from a ¼ strip half moon and a teat consisting of a ⅛ peg.

Mother and baby birds

The mother bird has a ½ strip teardrop body, a ¼ strip teardrop wing, a ¼ strip closed coil head (pulled to size) and a ⅛ strip teardrop beak. She is sitting on a ½ strip half-moon nest. The baby birds are each made from a ¼ strip teardrop body, a ⅛ strip teardrop wing, a ⅛ strip closed coil head and a ¹⁄₁₆ strip teardrop beak. The leaves are ¼ and ⅛ strip teardrops in various shades of green, and the buds are ⅛ strip teardrops.

When constructing the design, begin by assembling the birds on your quilling board, then glue down a length of green paper strip along its edge, then attach each of the elements, starting with the mother bird and working outwards.

Toys

Old-fashioned toys make us nostalgic for times gone by, and make wonderfully colourful decorations for children's greetings cards, party invitations and so on. The designs on these two pages can be tailored to the age of the child, for example by matching it to the number of carriages on the train or the number of yachts on the waves.

Jack-in-a-box

The jack-in-a-box can be quilled in as many different colours as you wish. Increase the length of his body, which consists of 1/2 strip squares, to make an unusual border. His arms are two 1/4 strip leaf shapes and his head is a full-strip closed coil. His hat is made of three triangles – one 1/2 strip and two 1/4 strips; the box is a full-strip red square; and the lid is a 1/3 strip marquise.

Toy rabbit

The rabbit's body is an eccentric coil consisting of a pink 1/2 strip joined in series with a white 1/2 strip. The tail is a 1/2 strip peg, the foot and arm are 1/4 strip teardrops, and the head is a full-strip closed coil. The ears are marquises made from a pink 1/4 strip joined in series with a white 1/4 strip, with the tips bent over. For the balloon, make a full-strip eccentric coil and attach a 1/8 strip triangle at the base.

Toy mouse

All children love a pull-along toy, and this little mouse will be no exception! His body is a full-strip teardrop with a 2cm (3/4in) tag left uncoiled for his tail. He has 1/8 strip pegs for both his nose and his eye. His ears are pink 1/8 strips joined in series to grey 1/8 strips and coiled into teardrops starting with the pink. The wheels are pegs made from black 1/8 strips joined in series with white 1/8 strips, coiled starting with the white. The string is a short length of paper strip glued along its edge.

Toy yachts

Each yacht has a hull made from a full-strip half moon and a 1/4 strip leaf-shape flag. The sails consist of a 3/4 strip and a 1/2 strip triangle. The waves are 1/3 strip scrolls made using graduated paper.

Toys and bricks

Each of the elements in this border, which I have arranged in a jumbled pile for a three-dimensional effect, could be used as separate motifs. The bricks, which are all ½ strip squares, are attached first, then the toys are glued on top.

The boat has ¼ strip triangular sails, a ⅛ strip teardrop flag and a ¼ strip marquise hull. The teddy bear has a ½ strip closed coil body and a ¼ strip closed coil head. His arms, legs and ears are all ⅛ strip teardrops, his ears then being shaped to fit around his head. The train and the carriage are ¼ strip squares, with wheels made of ¼ strip closed coils. The funnel is a ⅛ strip marquise.

Toy drum

This is made from two full-strip squares, with drumsticks consisting of ⅛ strips coiled into teardrops at one end. The musical notes are ⅛ strip pegs, with a tag left uncoiled and bent over at the end.

Doll

The doll's dress is a full-strip triangle and her head a 3 strip solid peg. Add in each strip after a few turns while coiling the peg by laying it over the end of the previous strip without gluing. Make the face more realistic by gently pushing the peg up into a dome shape. Strengthen the back of the head with a layer of PVA glue. The arms are ¼ strip pegs and the legs ¼ strip teardrops. Each plait is made from two ¼ strip teardrops with ⅛ strip triangles for bows. The top of her hair is a ½ strip teardrop. (See template on page 191.)

Toy train

The train can have as many carriages as you like. Perhaps spell out the child's name on the top of the carriages using sticker letters. The engine consists of four ½ strip squares with four ¼ strip closed coils for wheels. The funnel is a ¼ strip marquise, the boiler a ¼ strip half moon, and the smoke consists of ⅛ strip pegs. To assemble the engine, take a black ⅛ strip and coil a short length at each end into a peg. Leave a space in the centre long enough for the body and wheels. The carriages are two ½ strip squares with two ¼ strip closed coil wheels, and are assembled in the same way as the engine. The contents of each carriage are a mix of ⅛ strip pegs, ¼ strip pegs and ⅛ strip closed coils. The whole train is mounted on to a strip of paper glued flat on the background.

Templates

The templates on these pages are for the more complicated quilling designs shown on the preceding pages. Except where noted, they are all reproduced at full size.

*Speedwell Card (page 35) and
Wild Flower Sampler lower right
(pages 6–7).*

Scarlet Pimpernel Box (page 47).

Lesser Celandine Gift Bag (page 29). This template is reproduced at three-quarters of the actual size. You will need to enlarge it by 133 per cent on a photocopier.

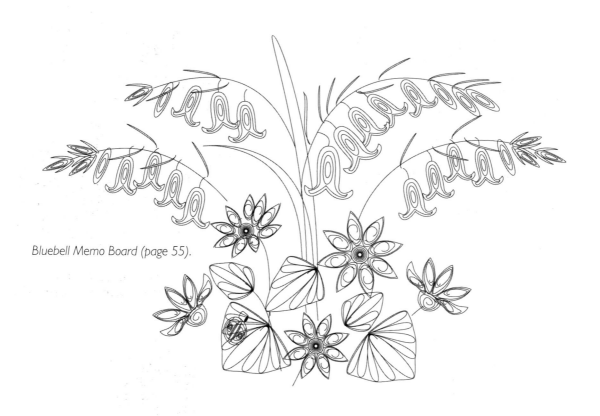

Bluebell Memo Board (page 55).

Lesser Celendine Card (page 29) and
Wild Flower Sampler upper right
(pages 6–7).

Sweet Violet Box front (page 41).

Sweet Violet Box top (page 41) and Wild Flower Sampler upper left (pages 6–7).

Sweet Violet Box left side (page 41).

Sweet Violet Box right side (page 41).

Sweet Violet Box back (page 41).

Peacock's body (page 152).

Yellow fantasy flower (page 164).

Blue fantasy flower (page 164).

Lilac fantasy flower (page 164).

Pink and green fantasy flower (page 164).

Daisy motif (page 164).

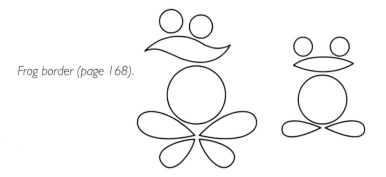

Frog border (page 168).

Peach butterfly (page 170).

Golden iris (page 169).

Blue and gold candle (page 172).

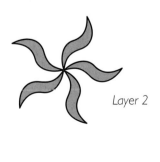

Poinsettia (page 173).

Layer 1

Layer 2

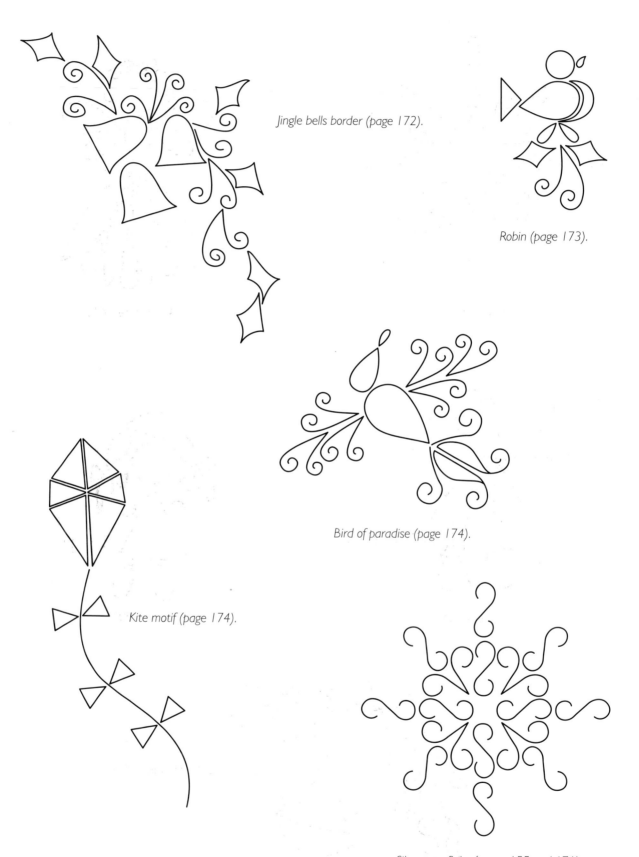

Jingle bells border (page 172).

Robin (page 173).

Bird of paradise (page 174).

Kite motif (page 174).

Silver snowflake (pages 155 and 176).